Set **A**

KEY STAGE 3
Levels 4–7

Reading Booklet

English

Food!

Letts

Contents

 Italy attempts to ban fake pizzas   page 3

 Oliver Twist   page 4

 Why is water good for you?   page 6

Pizza, from CBBC Newsround at bbc.co.uk/newsround, used with kind permission; How much water?, with thanks to Food Standards Agency © Crown Copyright foodstandards.gov.uk; Loch Ness Monster, http://crystalinks.com/loch_ness/html; Yeti, with kind permission of Lee Krystek © Lee Krystek unmuseum.org/bigfoot.htm; Jean Lafitte, with thanks to www.fact-index.com/j/je/jean_lafitte.html, © The text contained in Wikipedia is licenced to the public under the GNU Free Documentation Licence (GFDL). The full text of this licence is at Wikipedia:Text of the GNU Free Documentation License; Accordian Crimes, reprinted by permission of HarperCollins Publishers Ltd © E. Annie Proulx 1997; New Orleans,© 2004 Lonely Planet Publications. All rights reserved. Used with kind permission of www.lonelyplanet.com

Italy attempts to ban fake pizzas

1 Italy is planning to crack down on chefs making bad copies of pizza 'cos they're fed up with poor imitations.

2 The government wants strict rules on how a pizza should be made if it's to be called a Neapolitan pizza.

3 The new law will include a step-by-step guide to the perfect pizza, covering shape, depth, toppings and the way olive oil must be poured on top.

4 Pizza police will visit restaurants to make sure they stick to the rules, to guarantee their pizzas are genuine.

5 The rules about the pizza include:
   • must be round and no more than 35cm in diameter
   • must be cooked in a wood-fired oven
   • must be kneaded and shaped by hand
   • dough should be allowed to rise for at least six hours.

6 Top pizza chefs in Italy are delighted their famous food is going to be recognised and protected.

7 "Pizza is not just a food, it's a way of life," said pizza chef Vittorio Triunfo.

Made in Naples

8 Pizza is thought to have been invented in southern Italy in a place called Naples.

9 The famous Margherita was named after a queen of the same name and is topped with tomato, mozzarella and basil, the same colours as the Italian flag.

10 There are 23,000 pizzerias – special pizza restaurants – cooking up 56 million pizzas every year in Italy alone.

Oliver Twist

Oliver Twist is a young boy who is living in a kind of Victorian orphanage. The boys there are very badly treated and underfed. On this day, the boys decide that they want to be fed better …

1 Oliver Twist and his companions suffered the tortures of slow starvation for three months: at last they got so voracious and wild with hunger, that one boy, who was tall for his age, and hadn't been used to that sort of thing (for his father had kept a small cookshop), hinted darkly to his companions, that unless he had another basin of gruel, he was afraid he might some night happen to eat the boy who slept next him, who happened to be a weakly youth of tender age. He had a wild, hungry eye; and they implicitly believed him. A council was held; lots were cast who should walk up to the master after supper that evening, and ask for more; and it fell to Oliver Twist.

2 The evening arrived; the boys took their places. The master, in his cook's uniform, stationed himself at the copper; his pauper assistants ranged themselves behind him; the gruel was served out; and a long grace was said over the short commons. The gruel disappeared; the boys whispered to each other, and winked at Oliver; while his next neighbours nudged him. Child as he was, he was desperate with hunger, and reckless with misery. He rose from the table; and advancing to the master, basin and spoon in hand, said, somewhat alarmed at his own temerity:

3 "Please, sir, I want some more."

4　The master was a fat, healthy man; but he turned very pale. He gazed in stupefied astonishment on the small rebel for some seconds, and then clung for support to the copper. The assistants were paralysed with wonder; the boys with fear.

5　"What!" said the master at length, in a faint voice.

"Please, sir," replied Oliver, "I want some more."

6　The master aimed a blow at Oliver's head with the ladle; pinioned him in his arms; and shrieked aloud for the beadle.

7　The board were sitting in solemn conclave, when Mr. Bumble rushed into the room in great excitement, and addressing the gentleman in the high chair, said,

8　"Mr. Limbkins, I beg your pardon, sir! Oliver Twist has asked for more!"

9　There was a general start. Horror was depicted on every countenance.

10　"For more!" said Mr. Limbkins. "Compose yourself, Bumble, and answer me distinctly. Do I understand that he asked for more, after he had eaten the supper allotted by the dietary?"

11　"He did, sir," replied Bumble.

12　"That boy will be hung," said the gentleman in the white waistcoat. "I know that boy will be hung."

From *Oliver Twist* by Charles Dickens

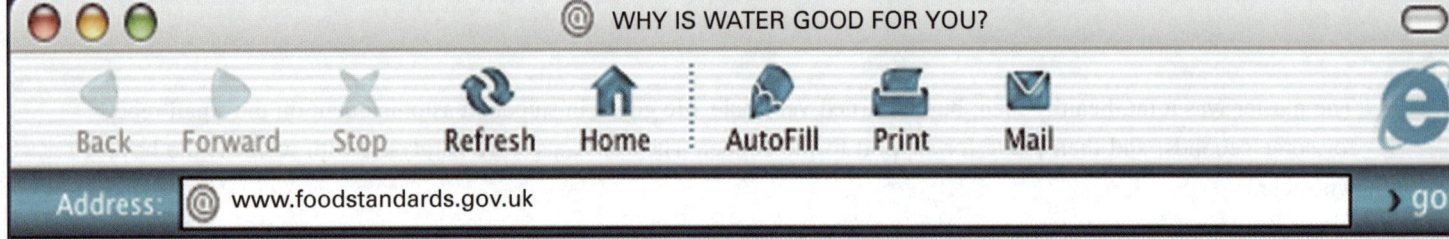

Address: www.foodstandards.gov.uk › go

@ Live Home Page @ Apple @ Apple Support @ Apple Store @ .Mac @ Mac OS X @ Microsoft MacTopia

Why is water good for you?

Why is it important to drink lots of water and how much should an adult drink each day?

1 Water is extremely important for our bodies to work properly. This is because water is responsible for moving nutrients around the body and most of the chemical reactions within our cells take place in water.

2 As your body works it produces waste products. Some of these waste products are toxic and the body gets rid of them through the kidneys in urine, which is mainly made up of water.

3 We also lose water by evaporation when we breathe and sweat. As the temperature rises and we do more activity, this increases the amount of water the body loses. To stay healthy, you need to replace the fluids that you lose.

4 In moderate climates, such as the UK, we should drink at least 6 to 8 cups/glasses of water (or other fluid) to prevent dehydration. In hotter climates your body will need more fluids.

5 Drinks that contain caffeine (such as tea, coffee and cola) can act as diuretics, which means they can make your body lose greater volumes of water than usual. So these drinks can lead to an increased need for water or other fluids that don't have a diuretic effect.

6 Drinks that contain sugar, such as fruit juice, some squashes and fizzy drinks, should also be drunk sparingly, because they can contribute to tooth decay. However, one glass of fruit juice can count towards the five portions of fruit and veg that we are recommended to eat each day.

Set A

KEY STAGE 3
Levels 4–7

Reading Test
Paper

English

Food!

Reading Test Paper

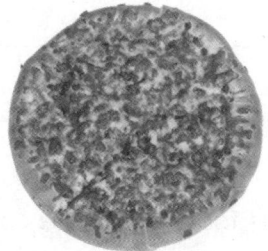

Food!

Instructions:

- find a quiet place where you can sit down and complete the test paper undisturbed

- make sure you have all the necessary equipment to complete the test paper

- read the questions carefully

- answer all the questions

- go through and check your answers when you have finished the test paper

Time:

This test paper is **1 hour 15 minutes** long.

You have **15 minutes** to read the Reading Booklet. During this time you are not allowed to open the Reading Paper to look at the questions.

You have **1 hour** to write the answers.

Write the answers in this booklet, then check how you have done against the mark scheme in the Answers Booklet.

Page	3	5	7	Max. Mark	Actual Mark
Score	....	....	....	32	....

First name ....

Last name ....

1   From the first three paragraphs, give two examples of what the Italian government wants to do.

(2 marks)

i _____

ii _____

2   a) In paragraph one, what does the choice of words in the following phrase suggest about the Italian government?

"Italy is planning to crack down on chefs making bad copies of pizzas"   *(1 mark)*

"crack down" suggests _____

_____

b) What do the words *"fed up"*, *"'cos"* and *"they're"* suggest about the writer's audience?

(1 mark)

_____

_____

3   a) The article is split into paragraphs with different topics. Complete this table by writing the correct paragraph number in the box next to the paragraph's topic.   *(2 marks)*

Topic	Paragraph Number
Rules about the pizza	
How the Margherita pizza got its name	
A reaction from a top pizza chef	
An introduction to the article	

b) Explain one reason why the text has paragraphs with personal comments as well as paragraphs about historical background.   *(1 mark)*

_____

_____

_____

4   How does the article try to appeal to young people?
     You should comment on the effect of:

- the language used

- the length of paragraphs

- the content of the article.   *(5 marks)*

5 a) From the first part of the first sentence, *"Oliver Twist and his companions suffered the
      tortures of slow starvation for three months"*, write down one word which suggests that the
      boys are suffering.   *(1 mark)*

      Q5a

_____

   b) What is the effect of this word?   *(1 mark)*

      Q5b

_____

_____

_____

_____

6   In the second sentence, it says *"He had a wild, hungry eye"*. What does the phrase "hungry
      eye" suggest about the boy's character?   *(1 mark)*

      Q6

_____

_____

_____

_____

7 a) From the whole text, identify one feature of Oliver Twist's character.   *(1 mark)*

      Q7a

_____

_____

_____

   b) From the whole text, identify one feature of the master's character.   *(1 mark)*

      Q7b

_____

_____

_____

8 a) The extract from the story begins with long paragraphs and ends with short paragraphs. Explain one reason why this is. *(1 mark)*

Q8a

_____

_____

_____

_____

_____

b) Explain how the line ' *"Please, sir," replied Oliver, "I want some more"'* makes you feel sorry for Oliver. *(1 mark)*

Q8b

_____

_____

_____

_____

_____

_____

9 What do you learn about the writer's viewpoint and purpose from the passage? Show whether the following statements are TRUE or FALSE by writing T for TRUE or F for FALSE in each of the boxes. *(2 marks)*

Q9

The writer wants us to feel sorry for Oliver. ☐

The writer is trying to criticise the way that boys like Oliver were treated by authority. ☐

The writer is trying to give a factual historical account. ☐

The writer is trying to entertain the reader. ☐

Turn over

subtotal

10   Explain two ways that the first paragraph gives us information. Support each explanation with a quotation.   *(2 marks)*   ☐ Q10

i   _____

_____

_____

ii   _____

_____

_____

11   How does the writer, in paragraphs three and four, try to convince the reader that drinking water is important? Choose two different words or phrases and explain how they create this effect on the reader.   *(2 marks)*   ☐ Q11

Word/Phrase	Effect on the reader	How it creates this effect on the reader
	makes the reader think that drinking water is important	because it suggests
	makes the reader think that drinking water is important	because it suggests

12 a) In paragraph five, what is described as the main effect of caffeine?   *(1 mark)*   ☐ Q12a

_____

_____

_____

b) Why are brackets used at the start of paragraph five in the phrase *"Drinks that contain caffeine (such as tea, coffee and cola)"*?   *(1 mark)*   ☐ Q12b

_____

_____

_____

13   In this web-page, how are language, grammar and content used to influence the reader?
      You should comment in your answer on the effect of the following.

      • The use of scientific words and phrases.

      • Sentence lengths.

      • The use of facts.   *(5 marks)*

Q13

_____

_____

_____

_____

_____

_____

_____

_____

_____

_____

_____

_____

_____

_____

_____

_____

_____

_____

                              END OF TEST

Set

A

KEY STAGE 3
Levels 4–7

Writing Test
Paper

English

Writing Test Paper

Food!

Instructions:

- find a quiet place where you can sit down and complete the test paper undisturbed

- make sure you have all the necessary equipment to complete the test paper

- read the questions carefully

- answer the questions on lined paper

- go through and check your answers when you have finished writing

Time:

This test paper is **1 hour 15 minutes** long.

You should spend **30 minutes** on the short writing task, including planning time.

You should spend **45 minutes** on the long writing task, including planning time.

Write the answers on lined paper, then check how you have done against the mark scheme in the Answers Booklet.

Short Writing Task

Strand	Max. Mark	Actual Mark
Sentence structure, punctuation and text organisation	6	
Composition and effect	10	
Spelling	4	

Long Writing Task

Strand	Max. Mark	Actual Mark
Sentence structure and punctuation	8	
Text structure and organisation	8	
Composition and effect	14	

First name ....

Last name ....

Writing Paper – Short Writing Task

Spend about 30 minutes on this section.

You write reviews for a school magazine – this week you have been asked to write a review of one of last week's school dinners.

Here is last week's menu.

Day	Main Course	Dessert
Monday	Fish and Chips	Ice-Cream
Tuesday	Cabbage Pie & Mashed Potatoes	Grapefruit Surprise
Wednesday	Broccoli & Cucumber Salad	Rhubarb Crumble
Thursday	Pizza	Melon Juice
Friday	Chicken Curry	Chocolate Sticky Pudding

In your review, the school magazine editor wants you to:

- analyse what was in the meal

- comment on what you thought about it.

Write your review on one of the school dinners above.

(20 marks, including 4 for spelling)

Writing Paper – Long Writing Task

Spend about 15 minutes planning your answer and 30 minutes writing.

Your local area has been named the least healthy in the whole country. You are a local newspaper journalist and you have been given the job of writing an article telling people about this and persuading them to adopt a more healthy lifestyle. Here are some of the facts that you have been given.

> 75% of the people in your area do not take regular exercise.
>
> 85% of the people in your area eat junk food, on average, four times a week.
>
> 60% of the people in your area visit the doctor once a month.
>
> The average life expectancy for men and women is five years below the national average.

Your editor wants you to write an article to:

- advise people about the situation in your area

- persuade them to change their ways.

Write the article!

(30 marks)

END OF TEST

Set
A

KEY STAGE 3
Levels 4–7

Shakespeare
Test Paper

English

Macbeth

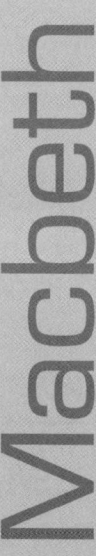

Shakespeare Test Paper

Macbeth

Instructions:

- find a quiet place where you can sit down and complete the test paper undisturbed

- make sure you have all the necessary equipment to complete the test paper

- read the question carefully

- answer the question on lined paper

- go through and check your answer when you have finished writing

Time:

This test paper is **45 minutes** long.

You are being tested on your reading and understanding of the Shakespeare scenes you have studied.

Check how you have done against the mark scheme in the Answers Booklet.

	Max. Mark	**Actual Mark**
Score	18	....

First name ....

Last name ....

Macbeth

You should spend about 45 minutes on this section.

Macbeth

Act 3 Scene 1 Line 113 – end of **Act 3 Scene 2**
Act 3 Scene 4 Lines 13 – 32

Macbeth, in these two extracts, is thinking a lot about his former
friend Banquo.

How do these extracts show Macbeth's attitude towards Banquo?

Support your ideas by referring to both of the extracts which are printed on the following pages.

(18 marks)

Use the printed scenes to answer the question set on page 3.

Act 3 Scene 1 Line 113 – end of **Act 3 Scene 2**

MACBETH
                                                                                Both of you
Know Banquo was your enemy.

Both Murderers
                                                                        True, my lord.

MACBETH
So is he mine; and in such bloody distance,
That every minute of his being thrusts
Against my near'st of life: and though I could
With barefaced power sweep him from my sight
And bid my will avouch it, yet I must not,
For certain friends that are both his and mine,
Whose loves I may not drop, but wail his fall
Who I myself struck down; and thence it is,
That I to your assistance do make love,
Masking the business from the common eye
For sundry weighty reasons.

Second Murderer
                                                                We shall, my lord,
Perform what you command us.

First Murderer
                                                                Though our lives–

MACBETH
Your spirits shine through you. Within this hour at most
I will advise you where to plant yourselves;
Acquaint you with the perfect spy o' the time,
The moment on't; for't must be done to-night,
And something from the palace; always thought
That I require a clearness: and with him–
To leave no rubs nor botches in the work–
Fleance his son, that keeps him company,
Whose absence is no less material to me
Than is his father's, must embrace the fate
Of that dark hour. Resolve yourselves apart:
I'll come to you anon.

Both Murderers
                                                        We are resolved, my lord.

MACBETH
I'll call upon you straight: abide within.

                                Exeunt Murderers

It is concluded. Banquo, thy soul's flight,
If it find heaven, must find it out to-night.

Exit

Scene 2. The palace.

Enter LADY MACBETH and a Servant

LADY MACBETH   Is Banquo gone from court?

Servant   Ay, madam, but returns again to-night.

LADY MACBETH   Say to the king, I would attend his leisure
For a few words.

Servant   Madam, I will.

Exit

LADY MACBETH   Nought's had, all's spent,
Where our desire is got without content:
'Tis safer to be that which we destroy
Than by destruction dwell in doubtful joy.

Enter MACBETH

How now, my lord! why do you keep alone,
Of sorriest fancies your companions making,
Using those thoughts which should indeed have died
With them they think on? Things without all remedy
Should be without regard: what's done is done.

MACBETH   We have scotch'd the snake, not kill'd it:
She'll close and be herself, whilst our poor malice
Remains in danger of her former tooth.
But let the frame of things disjoint,
both the worlds suffer,
Ere we will eat our meal in fear and sleep
In the affliction of these terrible dreams
That shake us nightly: better be with the dead,
Whom we, to gain our peace, have sent to peace,
Than on the torture of the mind to lie
In restless ecstasy. Duncan is in his grave;
After life's fitful fever he sleeps well;
Treason has done his worst: nor steel, nor poison,
Malice domestic, foreign levy, nothing,
Can touch him further.

Turn over

LADY MACBETH
                                        Come on;
Gentle my lord, sleek o'er your rugged looks;
Be bright and jovial among your guests to-night.

MACBETH
So shall I, love; and so, I pray, be you:
Let your remembrance apply to Banquo;
Present him eminence, both with eye and tongue:
Unsafe the while, that we
Must lave our honours in these flattering streams,
And make our faces vizards to our hearts,
Disguising what they are.

LADY MACBETH
                                You must leave this.

MACBETH
O, full of scorpions is my mind, dear wife!
Thou know'st that Banquo, and his Fleance, lives.

LADY MACBETH
But in them nature's copy's not eterne.

MACBETH
There's comfort yet; they are assailable;
Then be thou jocund: ere the bat hath flown
His cloister'd flight, ere to black Hecate's summons
The shard-borne beetle with his drowsy hums
Hath rung night's yawning peal, there shall be done
A deed of dreadful note.

LADY MACBETH
                                What's to be done?

MACBETH
Be innocent of the knowledge, dearest chuck,
Till thou applaud the deed. Come, seeling night,
Scarf up the tender eye of pitiful day;
And with thy bloody and invisible hand
Cancel and tear to pieces that great bond
Which keeps me pale! Light thickens; and the crow
Makes wing to the rooky wood:
Good things of day begin to droop and drowse;
While night's black agents to their preys do rouse.
Thou marvell'st at my words: but hold thee still;
Things bad begun make strong themselves by ill.
So, prithee, go with me.

MACBETH   There's blood on thy face.

First Murderer   'Tis Banquo's then.

MACBETH   'Tis better thee without than he within.
                           Is he dispatch'd?

First Murderer   My lord, his throat is cut; that I did for him.

MACBETH   Thou art the best o' the cut-throats: yet he's good
                           That did the like for Fleance: if thou didst it,
                           Thou art the nonpareil.

First Murderer   Most royal sir,
                           Fleance is 'scaped.

MACBETH   Then comes my fit again: I had else been perfect,
                           Whole as the marble, founded as the rock,
                           As broad and general as the casing air:
                           But now I am cabin'd, cribb'd, confined, bound in
                           To saucy doubts and fears. But Banquo's safe?

First Murderer   Ay, my good lord: safe in a ditch he bides,
                           With twenty trenched gashes on his head;
                           The least a death to nature.

MACBETH   Thanks for that:
                           There the grown serpent lies; the worm that's fled
                           Hath nature that in time will venom breed,
                           No teeth for the present. Get thee gone: to-morrow
                           We'll hear, ourselves, again.

END OF TEST

Set **A**

KEY STAGE 3
Levels 4–7

Shakespeare
Test Paper

English

Much Ado About Nothing

Shakespeare Test Paper

Much Ado About Nothing

Instructions:

- find a quiet place where you can sit down and complete the test paper undisturbed

- make sure you have all the necessary equipment to complete the test paper

- read the question carefully

- answer the question on lined paper

- go through and check your answer when you have finished writing

Time:

This test paper is **45 minutes** long.

You are being tested on your reading and understanding of the Shakespeare scenes you have studied.

Check how you have done against the mark scheme in the Answers Booklet.

	Max. Mark	**Actual Mark**
Score	18	....

First name ....

Last name ....

Much Ado About Nothing

You should spend about 45 minutes on this section.

Much Ado About Nothing

Act 1 Scene 1 Lines 139 – 175
Act 2 Scene 3 Lines 181 – end

In these two extracts the audience see Benedick acting very differently towards Beatrice.

Explain how these extracts would be quite amusing to the audience.

Support your ideas by referring to both of the extracts which are printed on the following pages.

(18 marks)

Act 1 Scene 1 Lines 139 – 175

CLAUDIO	Benedick, didst thou note the daughter of Signior Leonato?
BENEDICK	I noted her not; but I looked on her.
CLAUDIO	Is she not a modest young lady?
BENEDICK	Do you question me, as an honest man should do, for my simple true judgment; or would you have me speak after my custom, as being a professed tyrant to their sex?
CLAUDIO	No; I pray thee speak in sober judgment.
BENEDICK	Why, i' faith, methinks she's too low for a high praise, too brown for a fair praise and too little for a great praise: only this commendation I can afford her, that were she other than she is, she were unhandsome; and being no other but as she is, I do not like her.
CLAUDIO	Thou thinkest I am in sport: I pray thee tell me truly how thou likest her.
BENEDICK	Would you buy her, that you inquire after her?
CLAUDIO	Can the world buy such a jewel?
BENEDICK	Yea, and a case to put it into. But speak you this with a sad brow? or do you play the flouting Jack, to tell us Cupid is a good hare-finder and Vulcan a rare carpenter? Come, in what key shall a man take you, to go in the song?
CLAUDIO	In mine eye she is the sweetest lady that ever I looked on.
BENEDICK	I can see yet without spectacles and I see no such matter: there's her cousin, an she were not possessed with a fury, exceeds her as much in beauty as the first of May doth the last of December. But I hope you have no intent to turn husband, have you?

CLAUDIO	I would scarce trust myself, though I had sworn the contrary, if Hero would be my wife.
BENEDICK	Is't come to this? In faith, hath not the world one man but he will wear his cap with suspicion? Shall I never see a bachelor of three-score again? Go to, i' faith; an thou wilt needs thrust thy neck into a yoke, wear the print of it and sigh away Sundays. Look Don Pedro is returned to seek you.

Act 2 Scene 3 Lines 181 – end

DON PEDRO	And so will he do; for the man doth fear God, howsoever it seems not in him by some large jests he will make. Well I am sorry for your niece. Shall we go seek Benedick, and tell him of her love?
CLAUDIO	Never tell him, my lord: let her wear it out with good counsel.
LEONATO	Nay, that's impossible: she may wear her heart out first.
DON PEDRO	Well, we will hear further of it by your daughter: let it cool the while. I love Benedick well; and I could wish he would modestly examine himself, to see how much he is unworthy so good a lady.
LEONATO	My lord, will you walk? dinner is ready.
CLAUDIO	If he do not dote on her upon this, I will never trust my expectation.
DON PEDRO	Let there be the same net spread for her; and that must your daughter and her gentlewomen carry. The sport will be, when they hold one an opinion of another's dotage, and no such matter: that's the scene that I would see, which will be merely a dumb-show. Let us send her to call him in to dinner.

Exeunt DON PEDRO, CLAUDIO and LEONATO

BENEDICK	[*Coming forward*] This can be no trick: the conference was sadly borne. They have the truth of this from Hero. They seem to pity the lady: it seems her affections have their full bent. Love me! why, it must be requited. I hear how I am censured: they say I will bear myself proudly, if I perceive

Turn over

the love come from her; they say too that she will
rather die than give any sign of affection. I did
never think to marry: I must not seem proud: happy
are they that hear their detractions and can put
them to mending. They say the lady is fair; 'tis a
truth, I can bear them witness; and virtuous; 'tis
so, I cannot reprove it; and wise, but for loving
me; by my troth, it is no addition to her wit, nor
no great argument of her folly, for I will be
horribly in love with her. I may chance have some
odd quirks and remnants of wit broken on me,
because I have railed so long against marriage: but
doth not the appetite alter? a man loves the meat
in his youth that he cannot endure in his age.
Shall quips and sentences and these paper bullets of
the brain awe a man from the career of his humour?
No, the world must be peopled. When I said I would
die a bachelor, I did not think I should live till I
were married. Here comes Beatrice. By this day!
she's a fair lady: I do spy some marks of love in her.

Enter BEATRICE

BEATRICE   Against my will I am sent to bid you come in to dinner.

BENEDICK   Fair Beatrice, I thank you for your pains.

BEATRICE   I took no more pains for those thanks than you take
                    pains to thank me: if it had been painful, I would
                    not have come.

BENEDICK   You take pleasure then in the message?

BEATRICE   Yea, just so much as you may take upon a knife's
                    point and choke a daw withal. You have no stomach,
                    signor: fare you well.

Exit

BENEDICK   Ha! 'Against my will I am sent to bid you come in
                    to dinner;' there's a double meaning in that 'I took
                    no more pains for those thanks than you took pains
                    to thank me.' that's as much as to say, Any pains
                    that I take for you is as easy as thanks. If I do
                    not take pity of her, I am a villain; if I do not
                    love her, I am a Jew. I will go get her picture.

Exit

END OF TEST

Set
A

KEY STAGE 3
Levels 4–7

Shakespeare
Test Paper

English

Henry V

Shakespeare Test Paper

Henry V

Instructions:

- find a quiet place where you can sit down and complete the test paper undisturbed

- make sure you have all the necessary equipment to complete the test paper

- read the question carefully

- answer the question on lined paper

- go through and check your answer when you have finished writing

Time:

This test paper is **45 minutes** long.

You are being tested on your reading and understanding of the Shakespeare scenes you have studied.

Check how you have done against the mark scheme in the Answers Booklet.

	Max. Mark	**Actual Mark**
Score	18	....

First name ....

Last name ....

Henry V

You should spend about 45 minutes on this section.

Henry V

Act 4 Scene 1 Lines 220 – 280
Act 5 Scene 2 Lines 121 – 167

In these two extracts the audience learn a lot about the character of Henry.

How does Shakespeare show the audience that Henry is going to make a good king, in these two extracts?

Support your ideas by referring to both of the extracts which are printed on the following pages.

(18 marks)

Turn over

Act 4 Scene 1 Lines 220 – 280

BATES

Be friends, you English fools, be friends: we have
French quarrels enow, if you could tell how to reckon.

KING HENRY V

Indeed, the French may lay twenty French crowns to
one, they will beat us; for they bear them on their
shoulders: but it is no English treason to cut
French crowns, and to-morrow the king himself will
be a clipper.

Exeunt soldiers

Upon the king! let us our lives, our souls,
Our debts, our careful wives,
Our children and our sins lay on the king!
We must bear all. O hard condition,
Twin-born with greatness, subject to the breath
Of every fool, whose sense no more can feel
But his own wringing! What infinite heart's-ease
Must kings neglect, that private men enjoy!
And what have kings, that privates have not too,
Save ceremony, save general ceremony?
And what art thou, thou idle ceremony?
What kind of god art thou, that suffer'st more
Of mortal griefs than do thy worshippers?
What are thy rents? what are thy comings in?
O ceremony, show me but thy worth!
What is thy soul of adoration?
Art thou aught else but place, degree and form,
Creating awe and fear in other men?
Wherein thou art less happy being fear'd
Than they in fearing.
What drink'st thou oft, instead of homage sweet,
But poison'd flattery? O, be sick, great greatness,
And bid thy ceremony give thee cure!
Think'st thou the fiery fever will go out
With titles blown from adulation?
Will it give place to flexure and low bending?
Canst thou, when thou command'st the beggar's knee,
Command the health of it? No, thou proud dream,
That play'st so subtly with a king's repose;
I am a king that find thee, and I know
'Tis not the balm, the sceptre and the ball,

The sword, the mace, the crown imperial,
The intertissued robe of gold and pearl,
The farced title running 'fore the king,
The throne he sits on, nor the tide of pomp
That beats upon the high shore of this world,
No, not all these, thrice-gorgeous ceremony,
Not all these, laid in bed majestical,
Can sleep so soundly as the wretched slave,
Who with a body fill'd and vacant mind
Gets him to rest, cramm'd with distressful bread;
Never sees horrid night, the child of hell,
But, like a lackey, from the rise to set
Sweats in the eye of Phoebus and all night
Sleeps in Elysium; next day after dawn,
Doth rise and help Hyperion to his horse,
And follows so the ever-running year,
With profitable labour, to his grave:
And, but for ceremony, such a wretch,
Winding up days with toil and nights with sleep,
Had the fore-hand and vantage of a king.
The slave, a member of the country's peace,
Enjoys it; but in gross brain little wots
What watch the king keeps to maintain the peace,
Whose hours the peasant best advantages.

Act 5 Scene 2 Lines 121 – 167

KING HENRY V   The princess is the better Englishwoman. I' faith,
Kate, my wooing is fit for thy understanding: I am
glad thou canst speak no better English; for, if
thou couldst, thou wouldst find me such a plain king
that thou wouldst think I had sold my farm to buy my
crown. I know no ways to mince it in love, but
directly to say 'I love you:' then if you urge me
farther than to say 'do you in faith?' I wear out
my suit. Give me your answer; i' faith, do: and so
clap hands and a bargain: how say you, lady?

KATHARINE   Sauf votre honneur, me understand vell.

KING HENRY V   Marry, if you would put me to verses or to dance for
your sake, Kate, why you undid me: for the one, I
have neither words nor measure, and for the other, I
have no strength in measure, yet a reasonable
measure in strength. If I could win a lady at
leap-frog, or by vaulting into my saddle with my
armour on my back, under the correction of bragging

Turn over

be it spoken. I should quickly leap into a wife.
Or if I might buffet for my love, or bound my horse
for her favours, I could lay on like a butcher and
sit like a jack-an-apes, never off. But, before God,
Kate, I cannot look greenly nor gasp out my
eloquence, nor I have no cunning in protestation;
only downright oaths, which I never use till urged,
nor never break for urging. If thou canst love a
fellow of this temper, Kate, whose face is not worth
sun-burning, that never looks in his glass for love
of any thing he sees there, let thine eye be thy
cook. I speak to thee plain soldier: If thou canst
love me for this, take me: if not, to say to thee
that I shall die, is true; but for thy love, by the
Lord, no; yet I love thee too. And while thou
livest, dear Kate, take a fellow of plain and
uncoined constancy; for he perforce must do thee
right, because he hath not the gift to woo in other
places: for these fellows of infinite tongue, that
can rhyme themselves into ladies' favours, they do
always reason themselves out again. What! a
speaker is but a prater; a rhyme is but a ballad. A
good leg will fall; a straight back will stoop; a
black beard will turn white; a curled pate will grow
bald; a fair face will wither; a full eye will wax
hollow: but a good heart, Kate, is the sun and the
moon; or, rather, the sun, and not the moon; for it
shines bright and never changes, but keeps his
course truly. If thou would have such a one, take
me; and take me, take a soldier; take a soldier,
take a king. And what sayest thou then to my love?
speak, my fair, and fairly, I pray thee.

END OF TEST

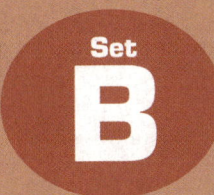

Set B

KEY STAGE 3
Levels 4–7

Reading Booklet

English

Monsters

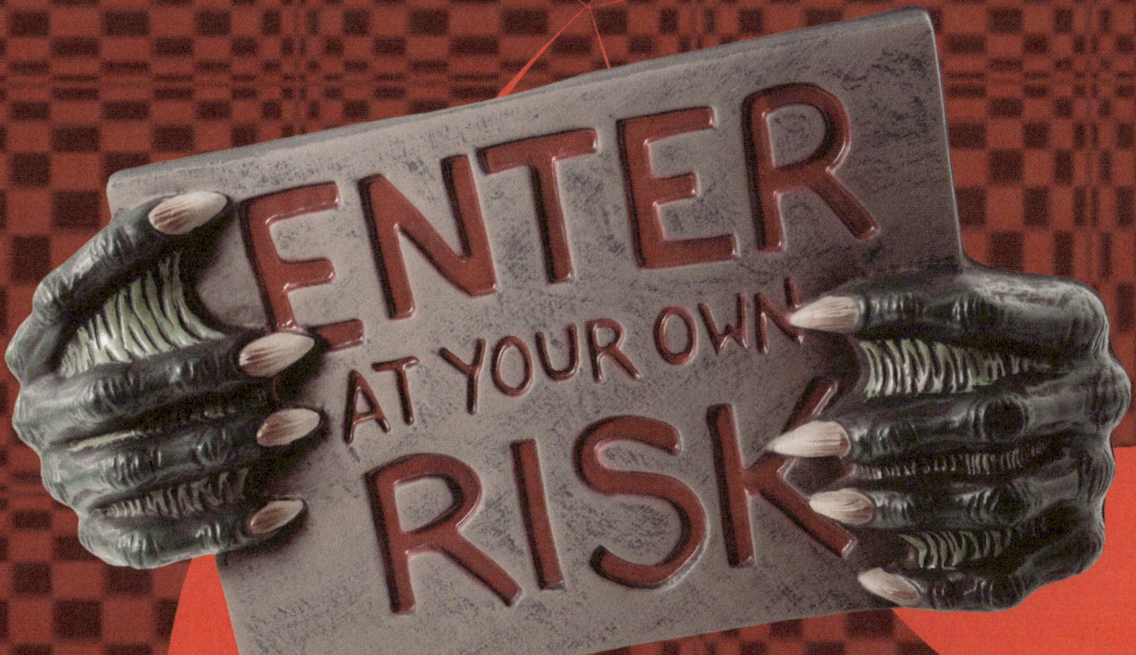
ENTER
AT YOUR OWN
RISK

Monsters

Letts

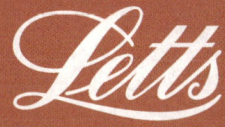

Contents

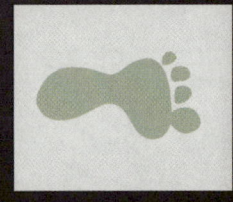 Bigfoot of North America

page 3

 Dracula

page 5

 The Loch Ness Monster

page 6

Bigfoot
of North America

1   If the Himalayas of Asia has its Yeti, the Pacific Northwest of America has its Bigfoot: a hairy, ape-like, biped that stands seven to nine feet tall and weighs between 600 and 900 pounds.

2   Bigfoot, or as it's often called in Canada, the *Sasquatch*, is mentioned in several native American legends. In fact, the term "Sasquatch" is Indian for "hairy giant". The first sighting of a Sasquatch footprint by a white man apparently came in 1811 near what is now the town of Jasper, Alberta, Canada. A trader named David Thompson found some strange footprints, fourteen inches long and eight inches wide, with four toes, in the snow.

3   In 1884 the newspaper, *Daily Colonist*, of Victoria, British Columbia, told of the capture of a "Sasquatch". The creature was spotted by a train crew along the Fraser River. The crew stopped the train, gave chase, and captured the animal after following it up a rocky hill. The creature was given the name "Jacko" and was "… something of the gorilla type, standing four feet seven inches in height and weighing 127 pounds. He has long, black, strong hair and resembles a human being, with one exception –

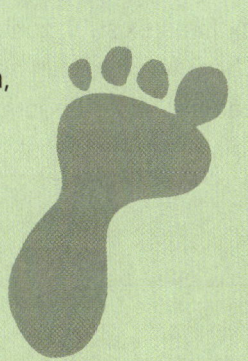

his entire body, excepting his hands (or paws) and feet, are covered with glossy hair about one inch long ... he possesses extraordinary strength, as he will take hold of a stick and break it by wrenching it or twisting it, which no man could break in the same way."

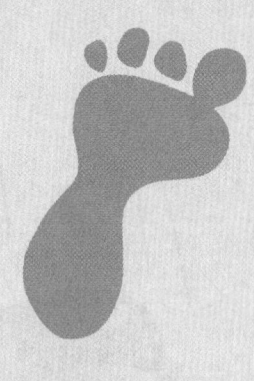

4   The description of Jacko is so much like that of a chimpanzee, and so unlike later Bigfoot reports, that some have suggested the animal actually was a chimpanzee. If brought back by a sailor from Africa, the animal might have escaped or been turned loose. There is also the strong possibility that the entire story was a hoax. Newspapers of that era often printed hoax stories to amuse their readers (perhaps not unlike some tabloids sold today).

5   Rumours about the Sasquatch continued through the end of the century. Then, in 1910, the murder of two miners, found with their heads cut off, was attributed to the creatures, though there was little supporting evidence that the killing wasn't human in origin. In any case, the place of the murders, Nahanni Valley, in Canada, was changed to Headless Valley, because of the incident.

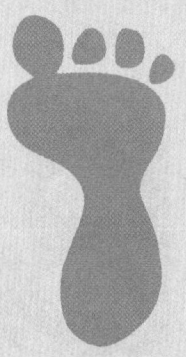

6   Interest in Bigfoot began to pick up in the United States in 1958 when a bulldozer operator named Jerry Crew found enormous footprints around where he was working in Humboldt County, California. Crew made a cast of the footprint. A local newspaper ran the story of Crew and his footprint with a photo. The story was picked up by other papers and ran throughout the country. It was the picture of Crew holding the "Bigfoot" that made the name stick.

7   In 1967 Roger Patterson and Bob Gimlin, Bigfoot buffs, announced they'd captured Bigfoot with a movie camera. They filmed a few seconds of an ape-like creature, apparently female, moving across a clearing near Bluff Creek in northern California. While the film is not perfectly clear, there is no mistaking the creature in the film for a common animal. The movie shows either a real Bigfoot, or a man in a clever costume. Nobody has ever proved the film fake, though some viewers were suspicious about the unnatural stride the creature had. One scientist who viewed the film, John Napier, of the Smithsonian Institution, admitted, "I couldn't see the zipper, and I still can't."

8   Scientists have a right to be suspicious of Bigfoot evidence. Two known hoax films exist. A controversial carcass, the "Minnesota Iceman", was thought to be a hoax, too. In addition, hoax footprints have been made from fake wooden feet and altered boots. One company even produced a set of oversized plastic strap-on feet that you could use to fool your friends and family.

With kind permission of Lee Krystek © Lee Krystek
unmuseum.org/bigfoot.htm

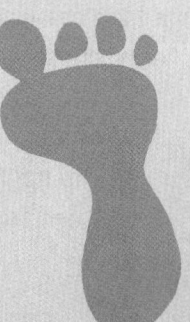

Dracula

1   **I** stood in silence where I was, for I did not know what to do. Of bell or knocker there was no sign. Through these frowning walls and dark window openings it was not likely that my voice could penetrate. The time I waited seemed endless, and I felt doubts and fears crowding upon me. What sort of place had I come to, and among what kind of people? What sort of grim adventure was it on which I had embarked? Was this a customary incident in the life of a solicitor's clerk sent out to explain the purchase of a London estate to a foreigner? Solicitor's clerk! Mina would not like that. Solicitor, for just before leaving London I got word that my examination was successful, and I am now a full-blown solicitor! I began to rub my eyes and pinch myself to see if I were awake. It all seemed like a horrible nightmare to me, and I expected that I should suddenly awake, and find myself at home, with the dawn struggling in through the windows, as I had now and again felt in the morning after a day of overwork. But my flesh answered the pinching test, and my eyes were not to be deceived. I was indeed awake and among the Carpathians. All I could do now was to be patient, and to wait the coming of morning.

2   Just as I had come to this conclusion I heard a heavy step approaching behind the great door, and saw through the chinks the gleam of a coming light. Then there was the sound of rattling chains and the clanking of massive bolts drawn back. A key was turned with the loud grating noise of long disuse, and the great door swung back.

3   Within, stood a tall old man, clean shaven save for a long white moustache, and clad in black from head to foot, without a single speck of colour about him anywhere. He held in his hand an antique silver lamp, in which the flame burned without a chimney or globe of any kind, throwing long quivering shadows as it flickered in the draught of the open door. The old man motioned me in with his right hand with a courtly gesture, saying in excellent English, but with a strange intonation.

4   "Welcome to my house! Enter freely and of your own free will!" He made no motion of stepping to meet me, but stood like a statue, as though his gesture of welcome had fixed him into stone. The instant, however, that I had stepped over the threshold, he moved impulsively forward, and holding out his hand grasped mine with a strength which made me wince, an effect which was not lessened by the fact that it seemed cold as ice, more like the hand of a dead than a living man.

From Chapter 2 of *Dracula* by Bram Stoker

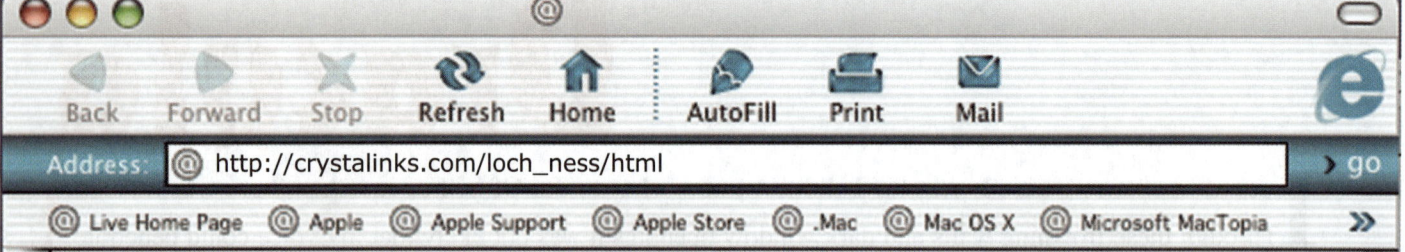

The Loch Ness Monster

1   The Loch Ness Monster is supposedly living in Scotland's Loch (Lake) Ness. "Nessie", as she is called, is the best known cryptozoological creature in the world.

2   Carvings of this unidentified animal, made by the ancient inhabitants of the Scottish Highlands some 1,500 years ago, are the earliest evidence that Loch Ness harbours a strange aquatic creature.

3   The earliest recorded sighting of the Loch Ness Monster was in the biography of St. Columba by Adamnan in the year 565 AD. The monster apparently attacked and killed a man who was swimming in the River Ness.

4   The monster didn't make headlines again until August 27, 1930 when 3 fishermen reported seeing a disturbance in the water. The men watched as a creature 20 feet long approached their boat throwing water in the air. As it passed them, its wake caused their boat to rock violently.

5   The men were convinced that the disturbance was caused by a living creature. Following the story, the newspaper received several letters from people claiming also to have seen a strange creature in the Loch.

6   In 1962, The Loch Ness Investigation Bureau was formed to act as a research organization and clearing house for information about the creature. In the beginning they only conducted research for a few weeks in the year, but by 1964 they established a more permanent presence around the Loch. Eventually the Bureau established camera stations with both still and cinema cameras with telephoto lenses. They had vans which served as mobile camera stations, and underwater listening devises. Searches were conducted using hot-air balloons and infrared night-time cameras, sonar scanners and submarines.

7   A great deal of information was discovered about the Loch, but they have yet to produce any concrete evidence of a monster.

8   Loch Ness is located in the north of Scotland and is one of a series of interlinked lochs which run along the Great Glen. The Great Glen is a distinctive incision which runs across the country and represents a large geological fault zone. The interlinking was completed in the 19th century following the completion of the Caledonian Canal.

9   The Great Glen is more than 700 ft (213 m) deep and ice free. It is fed by the Oich and other streams and drained by the Ness to the Moray Firth. It forms part of the Caledonian Canal. By volume, Loch Ness is the largest freshwater lake in Great Britain.

10 Since December 1933, when newspapers published accounts of a "monster", 40 to 50 ft (12–15 m) long, said to have been seen in the Loch, there have been alleged sightings.

11 As a result of the publicity, Loch Ness has become a major tourist attraction.

12 Several scientific studies have been conducted, including thorough sonar surveys of the Loch, and these have not revealed any presence of such a "monster".

13 Many people believe that the size and great depth of the Loch, together with potential underwater caves, gives the monster many places to hide.

14 Most of the Nessie witnesses describe something with two humps, a tail, and a snake-like head. A V-shape was often mentioned, as well as a gaping red mouth and horns or antennae on the top of the creature's head. Nessie's movements have been studied, and the films and photos analysed to determine what Nessie might be, if she exists.

15 There are numerous theories as to Nessie's identity, including a snake-like primitive whale known as a zeuglodon, a type of long-necked aquatic seal, giant eels, walruses, floating mats of plants, giant molluscs, otters, a "paraphysical" entity, mirages, and diving birds, but many lake monster researchers seem to favour the plesiosaur theory. The case has occasionally been supported by indistinct photographic evidence – though – in 1994 – a famous 1934 photograph was revealed to be a hoax.

Set B

KEY STAGE 3
Levels 4–7

Reading Test
Paper

English

Monsters

Reading Test Paper

Monsters

Instructions:

- find a quiet place where you can sit down and complete the test paper undisturbed

- make sure you have all the necessary equipment to complete the test paper

- read the questions carefully

- answer all the questions

- go through and check your answers when you have finished the test paper

Time:

This test paper is **1 hour 15 minutes** long.

You have **15 minutes** to read the Reading Booklet. During this time you are not allowed to open the Reading Paper to look at the questions.

You have **1 hour** to write the answers.

Write the answers in this booklet, then check how you have done against the mark scheme in the Answers Booklet.

Page	3	5	7	Max. Mark	**Actual Mark**
Score	....	....	....	32	....

First name _____

Last name _____

1   From paragraphs one and two, give two features of Bigfoot.   *(2 marks)*   Q1

     i _____

     ii _____

2   a) In paragraph two, what does the word "apparently" suggest in this sentence –
         "*The first sighting of a Sasquatch by a white man apparently came in 1811*"?   *(1 mark)*   Q2a

         The word "apparently" suggests _____

         _____

     b) In paragraph two, why does the writer refer to "*strange footprints*"?   *(1 mark)*   Q2b

         _____

         _____

         _____

3   a) Here are the topics of the first four paragraphs. Match up the topic with the correct
         paragraph number.   *(2 marks)*   Q3a

Topic	Paragraph Number
A description of a captured Sasquatch	
An introduction to what Bigfoot is	
An explanation of what the captured Sasquatch might have been	
The first sightings of a Sasquatch	

     b) Explain why the text has quotations about personal experiences as well as dates and facts.
         (1 mark)   Q3b

         _____

         _____

         _____

4   How does the writer make you feel that Bigfoot is probably a fake? You should comment on the effect of:

- the historical examples chosen

- the writer's comments on those examples

- the language used by the writer.   *(5 marks)*

Q4

_____

_____

_____

_____

_____

_____

_____

_____

_____

_____

_____

_____

_____

_____

_____

_____

_____

Turn over

5   a) From the first sentence, write down the phrase that shows the writer is confused.

(1 mark)

Q5a

_____

_____

_____

_____

   b) How does this phrase help to keep the reader's interest?   *(1 mark)*

Q5b

_____

_____

_____

_____

6   In the first paragraph, the writer describes *"these frowning walls and dark window openings"*.
    What does the word "frowning" suggest about the walls?   *(1 mark)*

Q6

_____

_____

_____

_____

7   a) From paragraph three, identify one thing about the old man that suggests he is well-mannered.

(1 mark)

Q7a

_____

_____

   b) From paragraph four, identify one thing about the old man that suggests he is unusual
      or strange.   *(1 mark)*

Q7b

_____

_____

8   a) Paragraphs one and two and paragraphs three and four are about different characters and are written in different styles.

Explain one difference in the way that they are written.   *(1 mark)*

_____

_____

_____

_____

_____

b) Explain how the fact that we don't know the old man's name at this point, or who he is, makes the story interesting.   *(1 mark)*

_____

_____

_____

_____

_____

9   What do you learn about the writer's viewpoint and purpose from the passage? Show whether the following statements are TRUE or FALSE by writing T for TRUE or F for FALSE in each of the boxes.   *(2 marks)*

The writer wants us to feel that the narrator is confident.   ☐

The writer's aim is to entertain and interest the reader.   ☐

The writer wants us to like the old man.   ☐

The aim of the writer is to build up tension in the reader.   ☐

Turn over

10   In the first two paragraphs, the writer gets the reader interested straight away by creating a
feeling of mystery.

Find two examples of where the writer does this and explain how each one makes the
article mysterious.   *(2 marks)*   Q10

i _____

   _____

ii _____

   _____

11   In paragraph five (from *"The men ..."* to *"..in the Loch."*) the writer tries to make the reader
feel that there might be some truth in the monster stories. Choose two different words or
phrases and explain how they create this effect on the reader.   *(2 marks)*   Q11

Word/Phrase	Effect on the reader	How it creates this effect on the reader
	makes the reader think that there might be some truth in the monster stories	because it suggests
	makes the reader think that there might be some truth in the monster stories	because it suggests

12 a) In paragraph twelve, it says *"Several scientific studies have been conducted, including
thorough sonar surveys of the Loch, and these have not revealed any presence of such a
"monster"*. Why does the writer use the word "thorough" in this sentence?   *(1 mark)*   Q12a

   _____

   _____

   b) Why is the word "monster" in inverted commas?   *(1 mark)*   Q12b

   _____

   _____

13   In this article, how does the writer use language and content to create a serious account about the monster?

You should comment on how the choice of content and language:

- makes the article sound scientific

- makes the article sound well researched

- includes a sense of mystery.

(5 marks)

Q13

_____

_____

_____

_____

_____

_____

_____

_____

_____

_____

_____

_____

_____

_____

_____

_____

_____

END OF TEST

subtotal

Set
B

KEY STAGE 3
Levels 4–7

Writing Test
Paper

English

Monsters

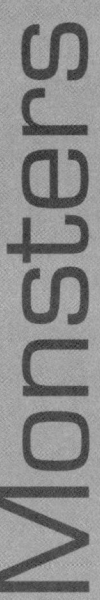

Writing Test Paper

Monsters

Instructions:

- find a quiet place where you can sit down and complete the test paper undisturbed

- make sure you have all the necessary equipment to complete the test paper

- read the questions carefully

- answer the questions on lined paper

- go through and check your answers when you have finished writing

Time:

This test paper is **1 hour 15 minutes** long.

You should spend **30 minutes** on the short writing task, including planning time.

You should spend **45 minutes** on the long writing task, including planning time.

Write the answers on lined paper, then check how you have done against the mark scheme in the Answers Booklet.

Short Writing Task

Strand	Max. Mark	Actual Mark
Sentence structure, punctuation and text organisation	6	
Composition and effect	10	
Spelling	4	

Long Writing Task

Strand	Max. Mark	Actual Mark
Sentence structure and punctuation	8	
Text structure and organisation	8	
Composition and effect	14	

Letts

First name ....

Last name ....

Writing Paper – Short Writing Task

Spend about 30 minutes on this section.

> You write ghost stories. You are about to start writing your next novel. The publisher wants you to write a convincing opening for your next story before they give you the money to go ahead and write it in full. The publisher wants you to write just the opening two or three paragraphs to show how you are going to get the reader's attention.

The publisher wants you to:

• Set the scene

• Create the mood

• End on a cliffhanger.

Write your opening, based on the ideas given above.

(20 marks, including 4 for spelling)

Writing Paper – Long Writing Task

Spend about 15 minutes planning your answer and 30 minutes writing.

Over the years, many people have reported sightings of ghosts and other supernatural events, but no one has been able to prove whether ghosts or other supernatural things actually exist or not.

Here are some reasons why people *don't* believe in ghosts and the supernatural.

• There is no scientific evidence to prove they exist.

• Often, they are witnessed by people alone, who could be making things up.

• Many of them have been proven to be fakes.

Here are some reasons why people *do* believe in ghosts and the supernatural.

• If only one of the thousands of cases is true, then they exist.

• There are many things that science cannot explain.

• People who have experienced them have been honest and trustworthy.

A Sunday magazine wants you to write an article arguing the case for and against ghosts existing, before you come to your own opinion. You can use the ideas above and any of your own ideas or examples, if you wish.

Write the article!

(30 marks)

END OF TEST

Set
B

KEY STAGE 3
Levels 4–7

Shakespeare
Test Paper

English

Macbeth

Shakespeare Test Paper

Macbeth

Instructions:

- find a quiet place where you can sit down and complete the test paper undisturbed

- make sure you have all the necessary equipment to complete the test paper

- read the question carefully

- answer the question on lined paper

- go through and check your answer when you have finished writing

Time:

This test paper is **45 minutes** long.

You are being tested on your reading and understanding of the Shakespeare scenes you have studied.

Check how you have done against the mark scheme in the Answers Booklet.

	Max. Mark	**Actual Mark**
Score	18	....

First name ....

Last name ....

Macbeth

You should spend about 45 minutes on this section.

Macbeth

Act 3 Scene 2 Line 4 – end
Act 3 Scene 4 Lines 49 – 107

We see that Macbeth is worried in these two extracts.

How do these extracts show Macbeth's state of mind?

Support your ideas by referring to both of the extracts which are printed on the following pages.

(18 marks)

Act 3 Scene 2 Line 4 – end

LADY MACBETH   Nought's had, all's spent,
                          Where our desire is got without content:
                          'Tis safer to be that which we destroy
                          Than by destruction dwell in doubtful joy.

                              Enter MACBETH

                          How now, my lord! why do you keep alone,
                          Of sorriest fancies your companions making,
                          Using those thoughts which should indeed have died
                          With them they think on? Things without all remedy
                          Should be without regard: what's done is done.

MACBETH   We have scotch'd the snake, not kill'd it:
                          She'll close and be herself, whilst our poor malice
                          Remains in danger of her former tooth.
                          But let the frame of things disjoint, both the
                          worlds suffer,
                          Ere we will eat our meal in fear and sleep
                          In the affliction of these terrible dreams
                          That shake us nightly: better be with the dead,
                          Whom we, to gain our peace, have sent to peace,
                          Than on the torture of the mind to lie
                          In restless ecstasy. Duncan is in his grave;
                          After life's fitful fever he sleeps well;
                          Treason has done his worst: nor steel, nor poison,
                          Malice domestic, foreign levy, nothing,
                          Can touch him further.

LADY MACBETH   Come on;
                          Gentle my lord, sleek o'er your rugged looks;
                          Be bright and jovial among your guests to-night.

MACBETH   So shall I, love; and so, I pray, be you:
                          Let your remembrance apply to Banquo;
                          Present him eminence, both with eye and tongue:
                          Unsafe the while, that we
                          Must lave our honours in these flattering streams,
                          And make our faces vizards to our hearts,
                          Disguising what they are.

LADY MACBETH   You must leave this.

MACBETH   O, full of scorpions is my mind, dear wife!
                     Thou know'st that Banquo, and his Fleance, lives.

LADY MACBETH   But in them nature's copy's not eterne.

MACBETH   There's comfort yet; they are assailable;
                     Then be thou jocund: ere the bat hath flown
                     His cloister'd flight, ere to black Hecate's summons
                     The shard-borne beetle with his drowsy hums
                     Hath rung night's yawning peal, there shall be done
                     A deed of dreadful note.

LADY MACBETH   What's to be done?

MACBETH   Be innocent of the knowledge, dearest chuck,
                     Till thou applaud the deed. Come, seeling night,
                     Scarf up the tender eye of pitiful day;
                     And with thy bloody and invisible hand
                     Cancel and tear to pieces that great bond
                     Which keeps me pale! Light thickens; and the crow
                     Makes wing to the rooky wood:
                     Good things of day begin to droop and drowse;
                     While night's black agents to their preys do rouse.
                     Thou marvell'st at my words: but hold thee still;
                     Things bad begun make strong themselves by ill.
                     So, prithee, go with me.

                                    Exeunt

Turn over

MACBETH	Which of you have done this?
Lords	What, my good lord?
MACBETH	Thou canst not say I did it: never shake Thy gory locks at me.
ROSS	Gentlemen, rise: his highness is not well.
LADY MACBETH	Sit, worthy friends: my lord is often thus, And hath been from his youth: pray you, keep seat; The fit is momentary; upon a thought He will again be well: if much you note him, You shall offend him and extend his passion: Feed, and regard him not. Are you a man?
MACBETH	Ay, and a bold one, that dare look on that Which might appal the devil.
LADY MACBETH	O proper stuff! This is the very painting of your fear: This is the air-drawn dagger which, you said, Led you to Duncan. O, these flaws and starts, Impostors to true fear, would well become A woman's story at a winter's fire, Authorized by her grandam. Shame itself! Why do you make such faces? When all's done, You look but on a stool.
MACBETH	Prithee, see there! behold! look! lo! how say you? Why, what care I? If thou canst nod, speak too. If charnel-houses and our graves must send Those that we bury back, our monuments Shall be the maws of kites.

GHOST OF BANQUO vanishes

LADY MACBETH	What, quite unmann'd in folly?
MACBETH	If I stand here, I saw him.
LADY MACBETH	Fie, for shame!
MACBETH	Blood hath been shed ere now, i' the olden time, Ere human statute purged the gentle weal; Ay, and since too, murders have been perform'd

Too terrible for the ear: the times have been,
That, when the brains were out, the man would die,
And there an end; but now they rise again,
With twenty mortal murders on their crowns,
And push us from our stools: this is more strange
Than such a murder is.

LADY MACBETH
                              My worthy lord,
Your noble friends do lack you.

MACBETH
                              I do forget.
Do not muse at me, my most worthy friends,
I have a strange infirmity, which is nothing
To those that know me. Come, love and health to all;
Then I'll sit down. Give me some wine; fill full.
I drink to the general joy o' the whole table,
And to our dear friend Banquo, whom we miss;
Would he were here! to all, and him, we thirst,
And all to all.

Lords
                    Our duties, and the pledge.

Re-enter GHOST OF BANQUO

MACBETH
Avaunt! and quit my sight! let the earth hide thee!
Thy bones are marrowless, thy blood is cold;
Thou hast no speculation in those eyes
Which thou dost glare with!

LADY MACBETH
                              Think of this, good peers,
But as a thing of custom: 'tis no other;
Only it spoils the pleasure of the time.

MACBETH
What man dare, I dare:
Approach thou like the rugged Russian bear,
The arm'd rhinoceros, or the Hyrcan tiger;
Take any shape but that, and my firm nerves
Shall never tremble: or be alive again,
And dare me to the desert with thy sword;
If trembling I inhabit then, protest me
The baby of a girl. Hence, horrible shadow!
Unreal mockery, hence!

GHOST OF BANQUO vanishes

END OF TEST

Set

B

KEY STAGE 3
Levels 4–7

Shakespeare
Test Paper

English

Much Ado About Nothing

Shakespeare Test Paper

Much Ado About Nothing

Instructions:

- find a quiet place where you can sit down and complete the test paper undisturbed

- make sure you have all the necessary equipment to complete the test paper

- read the question carefully

- answer the question on lined paper

- go through and check your answer when you have finished writing

Time:

This test paper is **45 minutes** long.

You are being tested on your reading and understanding of the Shakespeare scenes you have studied.

Check how you have done against the mark scheme in the Answers Booklet.

	Max. Mark	**Actual Mark**
Score	18	....

First name ....

Last name ....

Much Ado About Nothing

You should spend about 45 minutes on this section.

Much Ado About Nothing

Act 1 Scene 1 Lines 176 – 237
Act 2 Scene 3 Lines 81 – 144

In these two extracts Benedick is the subject of talk about his romantic life.

Explain how the audience might react to what is being said about Benedick and what he says in these two extracts, and why.

Support your ideas by referring to both of the extracts which are printed on the following pages.

(18 marks)

Act 1 Scene 1 Lines 176 – 237

DON PEDRO   What secret hath held you here, that you followed
                   not to Leonato's?

BENEDICK   I would your grace would constrain me to tell.

DON PEDRO   I charge thee on thy allegiance.

BENEDICK   You hear, Count Claudio: I can be secret as a dumb
                   man; I would have you think so; but, on my
                   allegiance, mark you this, on my allegiance. He is
                   in love. With who? now that is your grace's part.
                   Mark how short his answer is;–With Hero, Leonato's
                   short daughter.

CLAUDIO   If this were so, so were it uttered.

BENEDICK   Like the old tale, my lord: 'it is not so, nor
                   'twas not so, but, indeed, God forbid it should be
                   so.'

CLAUDIO   If my passion change not shortly, God forbid it   190
                   should be otherwise.

DON PEDRO   Amen, if you love her; for the lady is very well worthy.

CLAUDIO   You speak this to fetch me in, my lord.

DON PEDRO   By my troth, I speak my thought.

CLAUDIO   And, in faith, my lord, I spoke mine.

BENEDICK   And, by my two faiths and troths, my lord, I spoke mine.

CLAUDIO   That I love her, I feel.

DON PEDRO   That she is worthy, I know.

BENEDICK   That I neither feel how she should be loved nor
                   know how she should be worthy, is the opinion that
                   fire cannot melt out of me: I will die in it at the stake.

DON PEDRO	Thou wast ever an obstinate heretic in the despite of beauty.
CLAUDIO	And never could maintain his part but in the force of his will.
BENEDICK	That a woman conceived me, I thank her; that she brought me up, I likewise give her most humble thanks: but that I will have a recheat winded in my forehead, or hang my bugle in an invisible baldrick, all women shall pardon me. Because I will not do them the wrong to mistrust any, I will do myself the right to trust none; and the fine is, for the which I may go the finer, I will live a bachelor.
DON PEDRO	I shall see thee, ere I die, look pale with love.
BENEDICK	With anger, with sickness, or with hunger, my lord, not with love: prove that ever I lose more blood with love than I will get again with drinking, pick out mine eyes with a ballad-maker's pen and hang me up at the door of a brothel-house for the sign of blind Cupid.
DON PEDRO	Well, if ever thou dost fall from this faith, thou wilt prove a notable argument.
BENEDICK	If I do, hang me in a bottle like a cat and shoot at me; and he that hits me, let him be clapped on the shoulder, and called Adam.
DON PEDRO	Well, as time shall try: 'In time the savage bull doth bear the yoke.'
BENEDICK	The savage bull may; but if ever the sensible Benedick bear it, pluck off the bull's horns and set them in my forehead: and let me be vilely painted, and in such great letters as they write 'Here is good horse to hire,' let them signify under my sign 'Here you may see Benedick the married man.'
CLAUDIO	If this should ever happen, thou wouldst be horn-mad.
DON PEDRO	Nay, if Cupid have not spent all his quiver in Venice, thou wilt quake for this shortly.
BENEDICK	I look for an earthquake too, then.

Turn over

DON PEDRO

Come hither, Leonato. What was it you told me of to-day, that your niece Beatrice was in love with Signior Benedick?

CLAUDIO

O, ay: stalk on. stalk on; the fowl sits. I did never think that lady would have loved any man.

LEONATO

No, nor I neither; but most wonderful that she should so dote on Signior Benedick, whom she hath in all outward behaviors seemed ever to abhor.

BENEDICK

Is't possible? Sits the wind in that corner?

LEONATO

By my troth, my lord, I cannot tell what to think of it but that she loves him with an enraged affection: it is past the infinite of thought.

DON PEDRO

May be she doth but counterfeit.

CLAUDIO

Faith, like enough.

LEONATO

O God, counterfeit! There was never counterfeit of passion came so near the life of passion as she discovers it.

DON PEDRO

Why, what effects of passion shows she?

CLAUDIO

Bait the hook well; this fish will bite.

LEONATO

What effects, my lord? She will sit you, you heard my daughter tell you how.

CLAUDIO

She did, indeed.

DON PEDRO

How, how, pray you? You amaze me: I would have thought her spirit had been invincible against all assaults of affection.

LEONATO

I would have sworn it had, my lord; especially against Benedick.

BENEDICK

I should think this a gull, but that the white-bearded fellow speaks it: knavery cannot, sure, hide himself in such reverence.

CLAUDIO

He hath ta'en the infection: hold it up.

DON PEDRO	Hath she made her affection known to Benedick?
LEONATO	No; and swears she never will: that's her torment.
CLAUDIO	'Tis true, indeed; so your daughter says: 'Shall I,' says she, 'that have so oft encountered him with scorn, write to him that I love him?'
LEONATO	This says she now when she is beginning to write to him; for she'll be up twenty times a night, and there will she sit in her smock till she have writ a sheet of paper: my daughter tells us all.
CLAUDIO	Now you talk of a sheet of paper, I remember a pretty jest your daughter told us of.
LEONATO	O, when she had writ it and was reading it over, she found Benedick and Beatrice between the sheet?
CLAUDIO	That.
LEONATO	O, she tore the letter into a thousand halfpence; railed at herself, that she should be so immodest to write to one that she knew would flout her; 'I measure him,' says she, 'by my own spirit; for I should flout him, if he writ to me; yea, though I love him, I should.'
CLAUDIO	Then down upon her knees she falls, weeps, sobs, beats her heart, tears her hair, prays, curses; 'O sweet Benedick! God give me patience!'
LEONATO	She doth indeed; my daughter says so: and the ecstasy hath so much overborne her that my daughter is sometime afeared she will do a desperate outrage to herself: it is very true.
DON PEDRO	It were good that Benedick knew of it by some other, if she will not discover it.
CLAUDIO	To what end? He would make but a sport of it and torment the poor lady worse.

END OF TEST

Set B

KEY STAGE 3
Levels 4–7

Shakespeare
Test Paper

English

Henry V

Shakespeare Test Paper

Henry V

Instructions:

- find a quiet place where you can sit down and complete the test paper undisturbed

- make sure you have all the necessary equipment to complete the test paper

- read the question carefully

- answer the question on lined paper

- go through and check your answer when you have finished writing

Time:

This test paper is **45 minutes** long.

You are being tested on your reading and understanding of the Shakespeare scenes you have studied.

Check how you have done against the mark scheme in the Answers Booklet.

	Max. Mark	**Actual Mark**
Score	18	....

First name   ....

Last name   ....

Henry V

You should spend about 45 minutes on this section.

Henry V

Act 4 Scene 1 Lines 83 – 145
Act 5 Scene 2 Lines 98 – 175

In these two extracts the audience learn that Henry is worried about the job of a king.

How does Shakespeare show the audience the pressures that a king faces, in these extracts?

Support your ideas by referring to both of the extracts which are printed on the following pages.

(18 marks)

Use the printed scenes to answer the question set on page 3.

Act 4 Scene 1 Lines 83 – 145

SCENE I. The English camp at Agincourt.

Enter three soldiers, JOHN BATES, ALEXANDER COURT and MICHAEL WILLIAMS

COURT	Brother John Bates, is not that the morning which breaks yonder?
BATES	I think it be: but we have no great cause to desire the approach of day.
WILLIAMS	We see yonder the beginning of the day, but I think we shall never see the end of it. Who goes there?
KING HENRY V	A friend.
WILLIAMS	Under what captain serve you?
KING HENRY V	Under Sir Thomas Erpingham.
WILLIAMS	A good old commander and a most kind gentleman: I pray you, what thinks he of our estate?
KING HENRY V	Even as men wrecked upon a sand, that look to be washed off the next tide.
BATES	He hath not told his thought to the king?
KING HENRY V	No; nor it is not meet he should. For, though I speak it to you, I think the king is but a man, as I am: the violet smells to him as it doth to me: the element shows to him as it doth to me; all his senses have but human conditions: his ceremonies laid by, in his nakedness he appears but a man; and though his affections are higher mounted than ours, yet, when they stoop, they stoop with the like wing. Therefore when he sees reason of fears, as we do, his fears, out of doubt, be of the same relish as ours are: yet, in reason, no man should possess him with any appearance of fear, lest he, by showing it, should dishearten his army.

BATES	He may show what outward courage he will; but I believe, as cold a night as 'tis, he could wish himself in Thames up to the neck; and so I would he were, and I by him, at all adventures, so we were quit here.
KING HENRY V	By my troth, I will speak my conscience of the king: I think he would not wish himself any where but where he is.
BATES	Then I would he were here alone; so should he be sure to be ransomed, and a many poor men's lives saved.
KING HENRY V	I dare say you love him not so ill, to wish him here alone, howsoever you speak this to feel other men's minds: methinks I could not die any where so contented as in the king's company; his cause being just and his quarrel honourable.
WILLIAMS	That's more than we know.
BATES	Ay, or more than we should seek after; for we know enough, if we know we are the king's subjects: if his cause be wrong, our obedience to the king wipes the crime of it out of us.
WILLIAMS	But if the cause be not good, the king himself hath a heavy reckoning to make, when all those legs and arms and heads, chopped off in battle, shall join together at the latter day and cry all 'We died at such a place;' some swearing, some crying for a surgeon, some upon their wives left poor behind them, some upon the debts they owe, some upon their children rawly left. I am afeard there are few die well that die in a battle; for how can they charitably dispose of any thing, when blood is their argument? Now, if these men do not die well, it will be a black matter for the king that led them to it; whom to disobey were against all proportion of subjection.

Turn over

KING HENRY V   Fair Katharine, and most fair,
Will you vouchsafe to teach a soldier terms
Such as will enter at a lady's ear
And plead his love-suit to her gentle heart?

KATHARINE   Your majesty shall mock at me; I cannot speak your England.

KING HENRY V   O fair Katharine, if you will love me soundly with
your French heart, I will be glad to hear you
confess it brokenly with your English tongue. Do
you like me, Kate?

KATHARINE   Pardonnez-moi, I cannot tell vat is 'like me.'

KING HENRY V   An angel is like you, Kate, and you are like an angel.

KATHARINE   Que dit-il? Que je suis semblable à les anges?

ALICE   Oui, vraiment, sauf votre grace, ainsi dit-il.

KING HENRY V   I said so, dear Katharine; and I must not blush to
affirm it.

KATHARINE   O bon Dieu! Les langues des hommes sont pleines de
tromperies.

KING HENRY V   What says she, fair one? That the tongues of men
are full of deceits?

ALICE   Oui, dat de tongues of de mans is be full of
deceits: dat is de princess.

KING HENRY V   The princess is the better Englishwoman. I' faith,
Kate, my wooing is fit for thy understanding: I am
glad thou canst speak no better English; for, if
thou couldst, thou wouldst find me such a plain king
that thou wouldst think I had sold my farm to buy my
crown. I know no ways to mince it in love, but
directly to say 'I love you:' then if you urge me
farther than to say 'do you in faith?' I wear out
my suit. Give me your answer; i' faith, do: and so
clap hands and a bargain: how say you, lady?

KATHARINE   Sauf votre honneur, me understand vell.

KING HENRY V Marry, if you would put me to verses or to dance for your sake, Kate, why you undid me: for the one, I have neither words nor measure, and for the other, I have no strength in measure, yet a reasonable measure in strength. If I could win a lady at leap-frog, or by vaulting into my saddle with my armour on my back, under the correction of bragging be it spoken. I should quickly leap into a wife. Or if I might buffet for my love, or bound my horse for her favours, I could lay on like a butcher and sit like a jack-an-apes, never off. But, before God, Kate, I cannot look greenly nor gasp out my eloquence, nor I have no cunning in protestation; only downright oaths, which I never use till urged, nor never break for urging. If thou canst love a fellow of this temper, Kate, whose face is not worth sun-burning, that never looks in his glass for love of any thing he sees there, let thine eye be thy cook. I speak to thee plain soldier: If thou canst love me for this, take me: if not, to say to thee that I shall die, is true; but for thy love, by the Lord, no; yet I love thee too. And while thou livest, dear Kate, take a fellow of plain and uncoined constancy; for he perforce must do thee right, because he hath not the gift to woo in other places: for these fellows of infinite tongue, that can rhyme themselves into ladies' favours, they do always reason themselves out again. What! a speaker is but a prater; a rhyme is but a ballad. A good leg will fall; a straight back will stoop; a black beard will turn white; a curled pate will grow bald; a fair face will wither; a full eye will wax hollow: but a good heart, Kate, is the sun and the moon; or, rather, the sun, and not the moon; for it shines bright and never changes, but keeps his course truly. If thou would have such a one, take me; and take me, take a soldier; take a soldier, take a king. And what sayest thou then to my love? speak, my fair, and fairly, I pray thee.

KATHARINE Is it possible dat I sould love de enemy of France?

KING HENRY V No; it is not possible you should love the enemy of France, Kate: but, in loving me, you should love the friend of France; for I love France so well that I will not part with a village of it; I will have it all mine: and, Kate, when France is mine and I am yours, then yours is France and you are mine.

END OF TEST

Set C

KEY STAGE 3
Levels 4–7

Reading Booklet

English

Down South

Down South

Letts

Contents

 Jean Lafitte   page 3

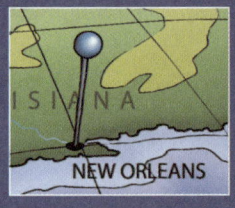 Arriving in New Orleans   page 4

 New Orleans   page 6

Jean Lafitte

1 Jean Lafitte or Laffite (*ca*1780 – *ca*1826?), was a pirate in the Gulf of Mexico in the early 19th century. He established his own "kingdom" of Barataria in the swamps and bayous near New Orleans after the Louisiana Purchase of 1803. He claimed to command more than 1000 men and provided them as troops for the Battle of New Orleans (1815). Afterwards he engaged in the slave trade after it had been banned.

2 Lafitte was a colourful character, said to have been born in France. He engaged in smuggling and privateering, with his "Kingdom of Barataria" (in what is now Louisiana) recognising the sovereignty of no other nation.

3 A controversial manuscript, known as the "Journal" of Jean Laffite, relates how, after his announced death in the 1820s, he lived in several states in the United States, raised a family and wrote this journal. At his request the publication of the journal was delayed for 100 years. In the 1950s the journal was translated from the French language and published. The original manuscript was purchased by Texas Governor Price Daniel and is on display at the Sam Houston Regional Library and Archives in Liberty, Texas.

4 Lafitte claimed never to have plundered an American vessel, and though he engaged in the contraband slave trade, he is accounted as a great romantic figure in Cajun Louisiana. His legend was perpetuated in Cecil B. DeMille's classic, *The Buccaneer* and even by a poem of Byron:

> *He left a corsair's name to other times,*
> *Linked one virtue to a thousand crimes.*

5 After the War of 1812, Lafitte or Laffite was active in the Neutral strip of coast between Spanish Texas and American Louisiana, left unoccupied and lawless until 1821.

6 His later years are obscure; a man many said was Lafitte died in Yucatan.

7 A U.S. National Park is named after him, in six physically separate sites in southeastern Louisiana, interpreting the local Acadian culture. The Barataria Preserve (in Jefferson Parish, Louisiana) interprets the natural and cultural history of the uplands, swamps, and marshlands of the region. Six miles southeast of New Orleans is the Chalmette Battlefield and National Cemetery, actual site of the 1815 battle and the final resting place for soldiers from the Civil War, Spanish – American War, World Wars I and II, and Vietnam.

8 **Jean Lafitte** is the name of a Cajun fishing village and tourist spot sited on Bayou Barataria.

With thanks to www.fact-index.com/j/je/jean_lafitte.html

Arriving in

1   They coasted into the delta, breathed its odour of mud and wood smoke under sunset clouds, gold curls combed out of the west, or the powdered stamens of a broad-throated flower. In the dusk they could see flickering lights in the side channels, sometimes hear a gruesome roar – the alligators, said a deckhand; no, a cow bogged in mud, said the woman with the nephews. The immigrants crowded the rail as the quivering ship moved into the Mississippi River, within the pincer of land. Silvano stood next to his father. A red moon crawled out of the east. On the shore the boy heard a horse snort. Hours before New Orleans the odour of the city reached them – a fetid stink of cesspools and the smell of burning sugar.

A demon in the backhouse

2   Nothing went as the accordion maker anticipated. The young man from the train was not at the dock. They waited hours for him while the other passengers disappeared into the teeming streets.

3   "True friends are as rare as white flies," said the accordion maker bitterly. Silvano gaped at the black men and especially the women, whose heads were wrapped in turbans as though they concealed emeralds and rubies and chains of gold beneath the winded cloth. They puzzled their way along the noisy, thronged streets with the young man's map and found Decatur Street, but there was no number 16 there, only charred timbers among rampant fireweed, a gap in the row of frowsty tenements. The accordion maker forced his courage, spoke to an approaching man who looked Sicilian; at least his hair appeared Sicilian.

4   "Excuse me, I seek a boardinghouse, number sixteen, but it seems there is no building here – " The man did not answer, spat to his right as he passed. Silvano saw the punishment for not knowing American. The man must be American – one who despised Sicilians ...

New Orleans

Back Forward Stop Refresh Home AutoFill Print Mail

Address: @ www.lonelyplanet.com › go

@ Live Home Page @ Apple @ Apple Support @ Apple Store @ .Mac @ Mac OS X @ Microsoft MacTopia

Favorites History Search Scrapbook Page Holder

INTRODUCTION

ORIENTATION

WHEN TO GO

EVENTS

ATTRACTIONS

OFF THE BEATEN TRACK

HISTORY

GETTING THERE & AWAY

GETTING AROUND

LONELY PLANET GUIDES

FURTHER READING

MAPS

New Orleans

1 New Orleans seduces with Caribbean colour and waves of sultry southern heat. Enshrouding us in dreams and ancient melodies, its sweet-tasting cocktails are laced with voodoo potions. The unofficial state motto, *laissez les bons temps rouler* ("let the good times roll"), pretty much says it all.

2 Called by some "The City That Care Forgot," New Orleans has a well-earned reputation for excess and debauchery. It's a cultural gumbo of African, Indian, Cajun and Creole influences. Whether you're looking for history, drama and intrigue or just a damn good bop in the street, New Orleans is it.

Area: 468 sq km
Population: 1.2 million
Country: USA
Time Zone: GMT/UTC -6 (Central Time)
Telephone Area Code: 504

BACK TO TOP

INTRODUCTION

ORIENTATION

WHEN TO GO

EVENTS

ATTRACTIONS

OFF THE BEATEN TRACK

HISTORY

GETTING THERE & AWAY

GETTING AROUND

LONELY PLANET GUIDES

FURTHER READING

MAPS

3   At the big toe of boot-shaped Louisiana, New Orleans nestles between Lake Pontchartrain, a huge but shallow body of saltwater that forms the northern edge of town, and a meniscus-shaped bend of the Mississippi River, about 145 river kilometres (90 miles) above where it empties into the Gulf of Mexico. The original and most visited portions of the city parallel the northern riverbank. Directions upriver or downriver are relative to the water flow, which bends maddeningly to all points of the compass. The Mississippi and Lake Pontchartrain also provide "riverside" or "lakeside" orientation.

4   New Orleans comprises a checkerboard of neighborhoods of different wealth and ethnicity – it's often only a few steps from ghetto to endowed estates. At the easternmost point of the city's crescent-shaped core is the heart of the original city, the French Quarter. To the southwest, the Uptown area encompasses the Garden District, universities and palatial mansions along the St Charles Ave Streetcar Line, which leads to the Riverbend area at the other end of the crescent.

5   Older *faubourgs* (suburbs) border the crowded French Quarter – to the east, the Faubourg Marigny appeals to a bohemian, mostly gay crowd, while the more down-at-heels Faubourg Tremé to the north is a black neighborhood known for its music. Downriver from Faubourg Marigny is the Bywater, a burgeoning artist hangout in an otherwise marginal district.

6   New Orleans International Airport (MSY) is 18 km (11 miles) west of the city center in Kenner, while both trains and buses share New Orleans Union Passenger Terminal ("Union Station") on Loyola Ave in the Central Business District (CBD), between the French Quarter and the Uptown area.

7   West of New Orleans you'll find the Cajun wetlands, an area of French patois-speaking rural people who still depend on the natural resources of the swamps. The Cajuns' Spanish counterparts, the Isleños, live in the coastal fishing villages south of New Orleans. Upstream along the Mississippi River, antebellum sugar plantations attract visitors who marvel at elegant plantation homes. An occasional slave cabin remains as a reminder of how the wealth was gained.

BACK TO TOP

Used with kind permission of www.lonelyplanet.com

Set **C**

KEY STAGE 3
Levels 4–7

Reading Test
Paper

English

Down South

Reading Test Paper

Down South

Instructions:

- find a quiet place where you can sit down and complete the test paper undisturbed

- make sure you have all the necessary equipment to complete the test paper

- read the questions carefully

- answer all the questions

- go through and check your answers when you have finished the test paper

Time:

This test paper is **1 hour 15 minutes** long.

You have **15 minutes** to read the Reading Booklet. During this time you are not allowed to open the Reading Paper to look at the questions.

You have **1 hour** to write the answers.

Write the answers in this booklet, then check how you have done against the mark scheme in the Answers Booklet.

Page	3	5	7	Max. Mark	**Actual Mark**
Score	....	....	....	32	....

First name _____

Last name _____

1   From paragraph one, give two different things that Jean Lafitte was well known for. *(2 marks)*

i _____

ii _____

2   In paragraphs two and four, what does the choice of words in the following phrases suggest about Jean Lafitte?

a) *"Lafitte was a colourful character"* *(1 mark)*

suggests _____

_____

b) *"he is accounted as a great romantic figure in Cajun Louisiana"* *(1 mark)*

suggests _____

_____

3   a) The article is split into a number of paragraphs. Each paragraph has a topic. Fill in the table with the missing paragraph numbers. *(2 marks)*

Topic	Paragraph Number
The end of Jean Lafitte's life	
Two places that exist today, connected to Jean Lafitte	
A summary of Jean Lafitte's main achievements	
The history of a diary about Jean Lafitte	
A place named after Jean Lafitte	
Reasons why Jean Lafitte became famous	

b) Give one reason why the text contains so many facts and very few opinions. *(1 mark)*

_____

_____

_____

4 How does the writer try to give the reader a fair view of the story of Jean Lafitte? You should comment on the effect of:

- The language used to describe Jean Lafitte and his life

- The use of facts and dates

- The content of the writing

(5 marks)

Turn over

5   a) From the sentence at the start of paragraph one, write down one word which suggests that
        the boat is moving slowly but effortlessly.   *(1 mark)*

        ☐ Q5a

    _____

    b) What does the word *"gruesome"* suggest in paragraph one?   *(1 mark)*

        ☐ Q5b

    _____

    _____

    _____

    _____

6   In paragraph one, the writer says *"The immigrants crowded the rail as the quivering ship
    moved into the Mississippi River ..."* What does the phrase *"crowded the rail"* suggest about
    the people?   *(1 mark)*

        ☐ Q6

    _____

    _____

    _____

    _____

    _____

    _____

7   From the whole text, identify two bad things about New Orleans.   *(2 marks)*

        ☐ Q7

    i   _____

        _____

        _____

    ii _____

        _____

        _____

8 a) This story is divided by a sub-heading: "*A demon in the backhouse*". Which event has the
       writer chosen to leave out and not describe, where the sub-heading is?   *(1 mark)*

_____

_____

   b) Explain how the first paragraph prepares us for the fact that the accordion maker's arrival in
      New Orleans was not going to be easy?   *(1 mark)*

_____

_____

_____

_____

_____

_____

9   What do you learn about the writer's viewpoint and purpose from the passage? Show whether
      the following statements are TRUE or FALSE by writing T for TRUE or F for FALSE in each of
      the boxes.   *(2 marks)*

The writer wants us to be aware that New Orleans is a smelly place.   ☐

The writer wants the reader to feel like the accordion maker.   ☐

The aim of the writer is to scare the reader.   ☐

The aim of the writer is to put people off visiting New Orleans.   ☐

Turn over

subtotal

10   The web-page begins *"New Orleans seduces with Caribbean colour and waves of sultry
      southern heat."*

      Explain two ways that this sentence makes the reader want to read more. Support each
      answer with a quotation from the sentence.   *(2 marks)*

      ☐ Q10

      i _____

        _____

      ii _____

        _____

11   Paragraph one, from *"Enshrouding us ..."* to the end of paragraph two, *"New Orleans is it,"*
      makes us feel that New Orleans is an exciting place but with a darker side. Choose two
      different words or phrases and explain how they create this effect on the reader.   *(2 marks)*

      ☐ Q11

Word/Phrase	Effect on the reader	How it creates this effect on the reader
	makes the reader think that New Orleans is exciting	because it suggests
	makes the reader think that New Orleans has a darker side	because it suggests

12   In the fourth paragraph, it says *"New Orleans comprises a checkerboard of neighbourhoods of
      different wealth and ethnicity"*.

   a) Why is New Orleans compared to a checkerboard?   *(1 mark)*

      ☐ Q12a

      _____

      _____

   b) In paragraph five, the word "suburbs" is in brackets. Why?   *(1 mark)*

      ☐ Q12b

      _____

      _____

13   How is language used in the whole text to make New Orleans sound like an exciting place
      to visit?

      You should comment on how the choice of words and phrases:

      • makes New Orleans sound lively

      • makes New Orleans sound mysterious

      • makes New Orleans sound historical and cultured.   (5 marks)

Q13

_____

_____

_____

_____

_____

_____

_____

_____

_____

_____

_____

_____

_____

_____

_____

                              END OF TEST

subtotal

Set C

KEY STAGE 3
Levels 4–7

Writing Test
Paper

English

Down South

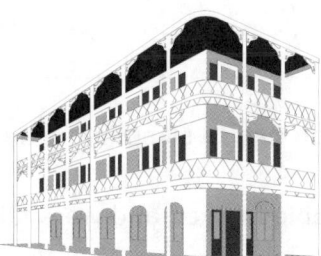

Writing Test Paper

Down South

Instructions:

- find a quiet place where you can sit down and complete the test paper undisturbed
- make sure you have all the necessary equipment to complete the test paper
- read the questions carefully
- answer the questions on lined paper
- go through and check your answers when you have finished writing

Time:

This test paper is **1 hour 15 minutes** long.

You should spend **30 minutes** on the short writing task, including planning time.

You should spend **45 minutes** on the long writing task, including planning time.

Write the answers on lined paper, then check how you have done against the mark scheme in the Answers Booklet.

Short Writing Task

Strand	Max. Mark	Actual Mark
Sentence structure, punctuation and text organisation	6	
Composition and effect	10	
Spelling	4	

Long Writing Task

Strand	Max. Mark	Actual Mark
Sentence structure and punctuation	8	
Text structure and organisation	8	
Composition and effect	14	

First name _____

Last name _____

Writing Paper – Short Writing Task

Spend about 30 minutes on this section.

You have just returned from a holiday which turned out to be a nightmare. The following things went wrong.

Your flights were delayed by 30 hours and you had to sleep in the airport lounge.

When you arrived, your rooms had been double-booked and were taken.

All your family got food-poisoning from the hotel's own food.

Write a letter to your local newspaper about what happened.

Analyse what went wrong and comment on the company you used.

You do not need to put any addresses – just start your letter with "Dear Sir or Madam".

Write the letter.

(20 marks, including 4 for spelling)

Writing Paper – Long Writing Task

Spend about 15 minutes planning your answer and 30 minutes writing.

Your local council have allocated a large part of their budget to attracting more tourists to your area. You are the council's publicity officer and it is your job to write the text for the brochure. You need to persuade tourists to visit your area.

In your brochure, you need to do these things.

- Tell people what your area has to offer them.

- Describe your area honestly, but make it sound as good as possible without telling lies!

- Sell your area to those people it might appeal to. Old or young? Single or married?

The council **DO NOT** need you to **design** the brochure – they **just** want you to write the text for it.

Write the text for your brochure.

(30 marks)

END OF TEST

Set
C

KEY STAGE 3
Levels 4–7

Shakespeare
Test Paper

English

Macbeth

Shakespeare Test Paper

Macbeth

Instructions:

- find a quiet place where you can sit down and complete the test paper undisturbed

- make sure you have all the necessary equipment to complete the test paper

- read the question carefully

- answer the question on lined paper

- go through and check your answer when you have finished writing

Time:

This test paper is **45 minutes** long.

You are being tested on your reading and understanding of the Shakespeare scenes you have studied.

Check how you have done against the mark scheme in the Answers Booklet.

	Max. Mark	**Actual Mark**
Score	18	....

First name ....

Last name ....

Macbeth

You should spend about 45 minutes on this section.

Macbeth

Act 3 Scene 1 Lines 91 – 139
Act 3 Scene 4 Lines 1 – 32

Macbeth talks to the Murderers in both of these extracts.

How do these conversations reveal Macbeth's attitude at this time in the play?

Support your ideas by referring to both of the extracts which are printed on the following pages.

(18 marks)

Act 3 Scene 1 Lines 91 – 139

First Murderer	We are men, my liege.

MACBETH

Ay, in the catalogue ye go for men;
As hounds and greyhounds, mongrels, spaniels, curs,
Shoughs, water-rugs and demi-wolves, are clept
All by the name of dogs: the valued file
Distinguishes the swift, the slow, the subtle,
The housekeeper, the hunter, every one
According to the gift which bounteous nature
Hath in him closed; whereby he does receive
Particular addition from the bill
That writes them all alike: and so of men.
Now, if you have a station in the file,
Not i' the worst rank of manhood, say 't;
And I will put that business in your bosoms,
Whose execution takes your enemy off,
Grapples you to the heart and love of us,
Who wear our health but sickly in his life,
Which in his death were perfect.

Second Murderer

I am one, my liege,
Whom the vile blows and buffets of the world
Have so incensed that I am reckless what
I do to spite the world.

First Murderer

And I another
So weary with disasters, tugg'd with fortune,
That I would set my lie on any chance,
To mend it, or be rid on't.

MACBETH

Both of you
Know Banquo was your enemy.

Both Murderers

True, my lord.

MACBETH

So is he mine; and in such bloody distance,
That every minute of his being thrusts
Against my near'st of life: and though I could
With barefaced power sweep him from my sight
And bid my will avouch it, yet I must not,
For certain friends that are both his and mine,

Whose loves I may not drop, but wail his fall
Who I myself struck down; and thence it is,
That I to your assistance do make love,
Masking the business from the common eye
For sundry weighty reasons.

Second Murderer   We shall, my lord,
Perform what you command us.

First Murderer   Though our lives–

MACBETH   Your spirits shine through you. Within this hour at most
I will advise you where to plant yourselves;
Acquaint you with the perfect spy o' the time,
The moment on't; for't must be done to-night,
And something from the palace; always thought
That I require a clearness: and with him–
To leave no rubs nor botches in the work–
Fleance his son, that keeps him company,
Whose absence is no less material to me
Than is his father's, must embrace the fate
Of that dark hour. Resolve yourselves apart:
I'll come to you anon.

Both Murderers   We are resolved, my lord.

Act 3 Scene 4 Lines 1 – 32

A banquet prepared. Enter MACBETH, LADY MACBETH, ROSS, LENNOX, Lords, and Attendants

MACBETH   You know your own degrees; sit down: at first
And last the hearty welcome.

Lords   Thanks to your majesty.

MACBETH   Ourself will mingle with society,
And play the humble host.
Our hostess keeps her state, but in best time
We will require her welcome.

LADY MACBETH   Pronounce it for me, sir, to all our friends;
For my heart speaks they are welcome.

First Murderer appears at the door

MACBETH   See, they encounter thee with their hearts' thanks.
Both sides are even: here I'll sit i' the midst:
Be large in mirth; anon we'll drink a measure

Turn over

The table round.

Approaching the door

There's blood on thy face.

First Murderer
'Tis Banquo's then.

MACBETH
'Tis better thee without than he within.
Is he dispatch'd?

First Murderer
My lord, his throat is cut; that I did for him.

MACBETH
Thou art the best o' the cut-throats: yet he's good
That did the like for Fleance: if thou didst it,
Thou art the nonpareil.

First Murderer
Most royal sir,
Fleance is 'scaped.

MACBETH
Then comes my fit again: I had else been perfect,
Whole as the marble, founded as the rock,
As broad and general as the casing air:
But now I am cabin'd, cribb'd, confined, bound in
To saucy doubts and fears. But Banquo's safe?

First Murderer
Ay, my good lord: safe in a ditch he bides,
With twenty trenched gashes on his head;
The least a death to nature.

MACBETH
Thanks for that:
There the grown serpent lies; the worm that's fled
Hath nature that in time will venom breed,
No teeth for the present. Get thee gone: to-morrow
We'll hear, ourselves, again.

Exit Murderer

END OF TEST

Set
C

KEY STAGE 3
Levels 4–7

Shakespeare
Test Paper

English

Much Ado About Nothing

Shakespeare Test Paper

Much Ado About Nothing

Instructions:

- find a quiet place where you can sit down and complete the test paper undisturbed

- make sure you have all the necessary equipment to complete the test paper

- read the question carefully

- answer the question on lined paper

- go through and check your answer when you have finished writing

Time:

This test paper is **45 minutes** long.

You are being tested on your reading and understanding of the Shakespeare scenes you have studied.

Check how you have done against the mark scheme in the Answers Booklet.

	Max. Mark	**Actual Mark**
Score	18	....

First name ....

Last name ....

Much Ado About Nothing

You should spend about 45 minutes on this section.

Much Ado About Nothing

Act 1 Scene 1 Lines 139 – 175
Act 2 Scene 3 Lines 148 – 223

In these two extracts we see a lot of Benedick.

What do the audience learn about the character of Benedick from these two extracts?

Support your ideas by referring to both of the extracts which are printed on the following pages.

(18 marks)

Turn over

Use the printed scenes to answer the question set on page 3.

Act 1 Scene 1 Lines 139 – 175

CLAUDIO   Benedick, didst thou note the daughter of Signior Leonato?

BENEDICK   I noted her not; but I looked on her.

CLAUDIO   Is she not a modest young lady?

BENEDICK   Do you question me, as an honest man should do, for
                 my simple true judgment; or would you have me speak
                 after my custom, as being a professed tyrant to their sex?

CLAUDIO   No; I pray thee speak in sober judgment.

BENEDICK   Why, i' faith, methinks she's too low for a high
                 praise, too brown for a fair praise and too little
                 for a great praise: only this commendation I can
                 afford her, that were she other than she is, she
                 were unhandsome; and being no other but as she is, I
                 do not like her.

CLAUDIO   Thou thinkest I am in sport: I pray thee tell me
                 truly how thou likest her.

BENEDICK   Would you buy her, that you inquire after her?

CLAUDIO   Can the world buy such a jewel?

BENEDICK   Yea, and a case to put it into. But speak you this
                 a sad brow? or do you play the flouting Jack,
                 to tell us Cupid is a good hare-finder and Vulcan a
                 rare carpenter? Come, in what key shall a man take
                 you, to go in the song?

CLAUDIO   In mine eye she is the sweetest lady that ever I
                 looked on.

BENEDICK   I can see yet without spectacles and I see no such
                 matter: there's her cousin, an she were not
                 possessed with a fury, exceeds her as much in beauty
                 as the first of May doth the last of December. But I
                 hope you have no intent to turn husband, have you?

CLAUDIO   I would scarce trust myself, though I had sworn the
                 contrary, if Hero would be my wife.

BENEDICK	Is't come to this? In faith, hath not the world one man but he will wear his cap with suspicion? Shall I never see a bachelor of three-score again? Go to, i' faith; an thou wilt needs thrust thy neck into a yoke, wear the print of it and sigh away Sundays. Look Don Pedro is returned to seek you.

Act 2 Scene 3 Lines 148 – 223

CLAUDIO	And she is exceeding wise.
DON PEDRO	In every thing but in loving Benedick.
LEONATO	O, my lord, wisdom and blood combating in so tender a body, we have ten proofs to one that blood hath the victory. I am sorry for her, as I have just cause, being her uncle and her guardian.
DON PEDRO	I would she had bestowed this dotage on me: I would have daffed all other respects and made her half myself. I pray you, tell Benedick of it, and hear what a' will say.
LEONATO	Were it good, think you?
CLAUDIO	Hero thinks surely she will die; for she says she will die, if he love her not, and she will die, ere she make her love known, and she will die, if he woo her, rather than she will bate one breath of her accustomed crossness.
DON PEDRO	She doth well: if she should make tender of her love, 'tis very possible he'll scorn it; for the man, as you know all, hath a contemptible spirit.
CLAUDIO	He is a very proper man.
DON PEDRO	He hath indeed a good outward happiness.
CLAUDIO	Before God! and, in my mind, very wise.
DON PEDRO	He doth indeed show some sparks that are like wit.
CLAUDIO	And I take him to be valiant.

Turn over

DON PEDRO	As Hector, I assure you: and in the managing of quarrels you may say he is wise; for either he avoids them with great discretion, or undertakes them with a most Christian-like fear.
LEONATO	If he do fear God, a' must necessarily keep peace: if he break the peace, he ought to enter into a quarrel with fear and trembling.
DON PEDRO	And so will he do; for the man doth fear God, howsoever it seems not in him by some large jests he will make. Well I am sorry for your niece. Shall we go seek Benedick, and tell him of her love?
CLAUDIO	Never tell him, my lord: let her wear it out with good counsel.
LEONATO	Nay, that's impossible: she may wear her heart out first.
DON PEDRO	Well, we will hear further of it by your daughter: let it cool the while. I love Benedick well; and I could wish he would modestly examine himself, to see how much he is unworthy so good a lady.
LEONATO	My lord, will you walk? dinner is ready.
CLAUDIO	If he do not dote on her upon this, I will never trust my expectation.
DON PEDRO	Let there be the same net spread for her; and that must your daughter and her gentlewomen carry. The sport will be, when they hold one an opinion of another's dotage, and no such matter: that's the scene that I would see, which will be merely a dumb-show. Let us send her to call him in to dinner.

Exeunt DON PEDRO, CLAUDIO, and LEONATO

BENEDICK

[*Coming forward*] This can be no trick: the
conference was sadly borne. They have the truth of
this from Hero. They seem to pity the lady: it
seems her affections have their full bent. Love me!
why, it must be requited. I hear how I am censured:
they say I will bear myself proudly, if I perceive
the love come from her; they say too that she will
rather die than give any sign of affection. I did
never think to marry: I must not seem proud: happy
are they that hear their detractions and can put
them to mending. They say the lady is fair; 'tis a
truth, I can bear them witness; and virtuous; 'tis
so, I cannot reprove it; and wise, but for loving
me; by my troth, it is no addition to her wit, nor
no great argument of her folly, for I will be
horribly in love with her. I may chance have some
odd quirks and remnants of wit broken on me,
because I have railed so long against marriage: but
doth not the appetite alter? a man loves the meat
in his youth that he cannot endure in his age.
Shall quips and sentences and these paper bullets of
the brain awe a man from the career of his humour?
No, the world must be peopled. When I said I would
die a bachelor, I did not think I should live till I
were married. Here comes Beatrice. By this day!
she's a fair lady: I do spy some marks of love in her.

END OF TEST

Set C

Shakespeare Test Paper

Henry V

Instructions:

- find a quiet place where you can sit down and complete the test paper undisturbed

- make sure you have all the necessary equipment to complete the test paper

- read the question carefully

- answer the question on lined paper

- go through and check your answer when you have finished writing

Time:

This test paper is **45 minutes** long.

You are being tested on your reading and understanding of the Shakespeare scenes you have studied.

Check how you have done against the mark scheme in the Answers Booklet.

	Max. Mark	**Actual Mark**
Score	18	....

First name ....

Last name ....

Letts

Henry V

You should spend about 45 minutes on this section.

Henry V

Act 4 Scene 1 Lines 112 – 183
Act 5 Scene 2 Lines 132 – 208

In these two extracts the audience learn that Henry has lots of problems to solve.

How does Shakespeare show the audience Henry's skills in solving the problems he is faced with?

Support your ideas by referring to both of the extracts which are printed on the following pages.

(18 marks)

Use the printed scenes to answer the question set on page 3.

Act 4 Scene 1 Lines 112 – 183

BATES	He may show what outward courage he will; but I believe, as cold a night as 'tis, he could wish himself in Thames up to the neck; and so I would he were, and I by him, at all adventures, so we were quit here.
KING HENRY V	By my troth, I will speak my conscience of the king: I think he would not wish himself any where but where he is.
BATES	Then I would he were here alone; so should he be sure to be ransomed, and a many poor men's lives saved.
KING HENRY V	I dare say you love him not so ill, to wish him here alone, howsoever you speak this to feel other men's minds: methinks I could not die any where so contented as in the king's company; his cause being just and his quarrel honourable.
WILLIAMS	That's more than we know.
BATES	Ay, or more than we should seek after; for we know enough, if we know we are the king's subjects: if his cause be wrong, our obedience to the king wipes the crime of it out of us.
WILLIAMS	But if the cause be not good, the king himself hath a heavy reckoning to make, when all those legs and arms and heads, chopped off in battle, shall join together at the latter day and cry all 'We died at such a place;' some swearing, some crying for a surgeon, some upon their wives left poor behind them, some upon the debts they owe, some upon their children rawly left. I am afeard there are few die well that die in a battle; for how can they charitably dispose of any thing, when blood is their argument? Now, if these men do not die well, it will be a black matter for the king that led them to it; whom to disobey were against all proportion of subjection.

KING HENRY V   So, if a son that is by his father sent about
merchandise do sinfully miscarry upon the sea, the
imputation of his wickedness by your rule, should be
imposed upon his father that sent him: or if a
servant, under his master's command transporting a
sum of money, be assailed by robbers and die in
many irreconciled iniquities, you may call the
business of the master the author of the servant's
damnation: but this is not so: the king is not
bound to answer the particular endings of his
soldiers, the father of his son, nor the master of
his servant; for they purpose not their death, when
they purpose their services. Besides, there is no
king, be his cause never so spotless, if it come to
the arbitrement of swords, can try it out with all
unspotted soldiers: some peradventure have on them
the guilt of premeditated and contrived murder;
some, of beguiling virgins with the broken seals of
perjury; some, making the wars their bulwark, that
have before gored the gentle bosom of peace with
pillage and robbery. Now, if these men have
defeated the law and outrun native punishment,
though they can outstrip men, they have no wings to
fly from God: war is his beadle, war is vengeance;
so that here men are punished for before-breach of
the king's laws in now the king's quarrel: where
they feared the death, they have borne life away;
and where they would be safe, they perish: then if
they die unprovided, no more is the king guilty of
their damnation than he was before guilty of those
impieties for the which they are now visited. Every
subject's duty is the king's; but every subject's
soul is his own. Therefore should every soldier in
the wars do as every sick man in his bed, wash every
mote out of his conscience: and dying so, death
is to him advantage; or not dying, the time was
blessedly lost wherein such preparation was gained:
and in him that escapes, it were not sin to think
that, making God so free an offer, He let him
outlive that day to see His greatness and to teach
others how they should prepare.

Turn over

KING HENRY V

Marry, if you would put me to verses or to dance for your sake, Kate, why you undid me: for the one, I have neither words nor measure, and for the other, I have no strength in measure, yet a reasonable measure in strength. If I could win a lady at leap-frog, or by vaulting into my saddle with my armour on my back, under the correction of bragging be it spoken. I should quickly leap into a wife. Or if I might buffet for my love, or bound my horse for her favours, I could lay on like a butcher and sit like a jack-an-apes, never off. But, before God, Kate, I cannot look greenly nor gasp out my eloquence, nor I have no cunning in protestation; only downright oaths, which I never use till urged, nor never break for urging. If thou canst love a fellow of this temper, Kate, whose face is not worth sun-burning, that never looks in his glass for love of any thing he sees there, let thine eye be thy cook. I speak to thee plain soldier: If thou canst love me for this, take me: if not, to say to thee that I shall die, is true; but for thy love, by the Lord, no; yet I love thee too. And while thou livest, dear Kate, take a fellow of plain and uncoined constancy; for he perforce must do thee right, because he hath not the gift to woo in other places: for these fellows of infinite tongue, that can rhyme themselves into ladies' favours, they do always reason themselves out again. What! a speaker is but a prater; a rhyme is but a ballad. A good leg will fall; a straight back will stoop; a black beard will turn white; a curled pate will grow bald; a fair face will wither; a full eye will wax hollow: but a good heart, Kate, is the sun and the moon; or, rather, the sun, and not the moon; for it shines bright and never changes, but keeps his course truly. If thou would have such a one, take me; and take me, take a soldier; take a soldier, take a king. And what sayest thou then to my love? speak, my fair, and fairly, I pray thee.

KATHARINE

Is it possible dat I sould love de enemy of France?

KING HENRY V	No; it is not possible you should love the enemy of France, Kate: but, in loving me, you should love the friend of France; for I love France so well that I will not part with a village of it; I will have it all mine: and, Kate, when France is mine and I am yours, then yours is France and you are mine.
KATHARINE	I cannot tell vat is dat.
KING HENRY V	No, Kate? I will tell thee in French; which I am sure will hang upon my tongue like a new-married wife about her husband's neck, hardly to be shook off. Je quand sur le possession de France, et quand vous avez le possession de moi,–let me see, what then? Saint Denis be my speed!–donc votre est France et vous êtes mienne. It is as easy for me, Kate, to conquer the kingdom as to speak so much more French: I shall never move thee in French, unless it be to laugh at me.
KATHARINE	Sauf votre honneur, le Francois que vous parlez, il est meilleur que l'Anglois lequel je parle.
KING HENRY V	No, faith, is't not, Kate: but thy speaking of my tongue, and I thine, most truly-falsely, must needs be granted to be much at one. But, Kate, dost thou understand thus much English, canst thou love me?
KATHARINE	I cannot tell.
KING HENRY V	Can any of your neighbours tell, Kate? I'll ask them. Come, I know thou lovest me: and at night, when you come into your closet, you'll question this gentlewoman about me; and I know, Kate, you will to her dispraise those parts in me that you love with your heart: but, good Kate, mock me mercifully; the rather, gentle princess, because I love thee cruelly. If ever thou beest mine, Kate, as I have a saving faith within me tells me thou shalt, I get thee with scambling, and thou must therefore needs prove a good soldier-breeder: shall not thou and I, between Saint Denis and Saint George, compound a boy, half French, half English, that shall go to Constantinople and take the Turk by the beard? shall we not? what sayest thou, my fair flower-de-luce?

END OF TEST

Sets

ABC

KEY STAGE 3
Levels 4–7

Answers,
Mark Scheme &
Advice Booklet

English

Answers

Answers, Mark Scheme & Advice Booklet

This booklet provides advice on how to approach the SATs questions, as well as supplying the answers and the mark schemes for each of the Test Papers.

On page 4, there is a grid to record your marks in and a guide showing how your marks relate to levels.

Contents

- Advice — page 2
- Mark and Level Grid — page 4
- Set A Answers – "Food!" Reading Test Paper — page 5
- Set B Answers – "Monsters" Reading Test Paper — page 8
- Set C Answers – "Down South"' Reading Test Paper — page 11
- Writing Test Papers — page 14
- Long Writing Task Papers – Mark Scheme — page 14
- Short Writing Task Papers – Mark Scheme — page 17
- Shakespeare Test Papers – Mark Scheme — page 19

Advice

Short answer questions

These questions test a range of different skills.
You will do well on this test paper by thinking about a number of things.

1   Organise your time. People who do well on this paper make sure that they spend an appropriate amount of time on each question. There are 32 marks for this paper, and you have one hour to write your answers, so you should be spending just under 2 minutes on each mark. Stick to this. If you get stuck, move on and come back to the missed questions at the end, if you have time.

2   Know what the questions require. The questions are testing different reading skills. Some require short answers, others need examples and some require a mixture. Obviously, the number of marks available and the amount of space for the answer gives some idea of how much to write, but you should also know what the different instruction words in the questions mean. Here is a range of commonly used instruction words used in this paper and what they require from you.

   "Give reasons" – explain – put things in your own words.
   "What does ... suggest?" – give your own personal opinion based on the way the word is used in the text.
   "Explain" – what it says! Use your own words.
   "Identify" – give an example, or a quotation.
   "What is the effect of ...?" – give your own personal opinion based on the way the word is used in the text.
   "Why is ...?" – explain – put things in your own words.

3   When filling in charts and boxes, don't put more answers than you are allowed. You will simply be given zero!

4   On the questions worth 5 marks, make sure you have a quotation and a comment on every bullet point. To get the top marks on the 5 marks questions, pick out individual words from your quotations and use those individual words to show exactly where you have got your ideas from.

The writing tasks

In school, all through KS3, you will have learnt about different styles of writing. The long and short writing tasks are testing to see if you know how to write in different styles. This means the following.

1   Revise what you have learnt in school about how to write in different styles, e.g. How do you write to:
   • imagine, explore, entertain
   • argue, persuade, advise
   • inform, explain, describe
   • analyse, review, comment?

   If you revise what you have done on each of these writing types, then it will help you to get more marks for "Communication and effect" which carries the most marks on both the long and short tasks.

2   Plan your answer! If you want to get good marks for paragraphing and organisation, then it is essential to do a short plan first. It doesn't matter how you plan – you could brainstorm, mind map – do whatever suits your learning style. At the very least, decide what will happen in the beginning, middle and end of your writing. If you have time, decide what you are going to put in each paragraph.

3   Leave a short amount of time to proof-read what you have written. On the short task, make sure you check spelling, because you gain marks for "Spelling" on that task.

4   You don't have to worry about writing vast amounts, especially on the short answer task. The marker is looking for quality, not quantity.

The Shakespeare papers

Before you do a paper as follows:

- make sure that you understand what is **happening** in your scenes **first**
- make sure that you know what the **important quotations** are in your scenes – what they **are**, what they **mean** and how you might **explain** them
- know how your scenes **relate to the rest of the play**.

In the SATs exam you should do the following:

1   Read the question carefully.

2   Write on the question paper – underline the key words in the question. Use these to identify what you have to include in your answer. A highlighter pen would be handy!

3   Use the words you have underlined in the question to help identify the quotations you are going to use from the extracts. Remember that the extracts given to you are only about half of the scenes you have studied. Again, a highlighter pen would be useful.

4   Plan your answer – make sure you cover all parts of the question required.

5   You can refer to other parts of the play, and probably will, but only do so in passing – there won't be time for you to answer the question properly if you focus on too much outside the set scenes. Use a quotation for every point you make. Pick words out of the quotations where possible, because you will show more exactly where you have got your ideas from, which is essential to get Level 6 and Level 7.

6   To show your personal opinion on the language of the play, pick out words and use sentences like "the word … suggests to me … because …", "the words ... imply that … because …". Frame your comments using sentence frames like these and you will be showing personal opinion and developing your ideas in depth, which should mean that you are commenting at least at Level 5 or above, depending on how thoroughly and sensibly you phrase your comments.

7   Make sure that you answer on both scenes. If you only answer on one scene, then the marker will mark your answer and drop your marks by one band in the mark scheme. This could mean you dropping a level on your overall Reading score, so manage your time carefully.

Mark and Level Grid

Enter your scores in the grid below and then work out your level using the mark ranges at the bottom of the page.

To work out your Reading level, add your scores for the Reading Test Paper short answer questions and the Shakespeare Test Paper. Make a note of your score in the table below and use the chart at the bottom of the page to find your level.

To work out your Writing level, add your scores for the short and long writing tasks. Make a note of your score in the table below and use the chart at the bottom of the page to find your level.

To find your overall level, add together your total Reading and Writing scores. Make a note of your score in the table below and use the chart at the bottom of the page to find your level.

Paper	Set A	Set B	Set C
Reading Test Paper – short answer questions			
Shakespeare Test Paper			
Reading total			
Reading level			
Short writing task			
Long writing task			
Writing total			
Writing level			
Total			

To find your Reading, Writing and Overall levels, use the charts below.

Level	Reading mark range	Writing mark range	Overall
No level	Below 8	Below 5	0 – 10
3	8 – 10	5 – 10	11 – 15
4	11 – 16	11 – 12	16 – 30
5	17 – 26	13 – 22	31 – 50
6	27 – 33	23 – 31	51 – 65
7	34 – 50	32 – 50	66 – 100

Set A Answers – "Food!" Reading Test Paper

Italy attempts to ban fake pizzas

1   It wants to crack down on chefs making bad copies of pizzas.
It wants to create strict rules about pizza making.
It wants a step-by-step guide to pizza making.

(1 mark for each different response, up to a maximum of 2 marks)

2   a) It suggests that they want to take extreme/firm/forceful action about the problem.   *(1 mark)*

     b) They suggest that the audience is one which accepts informal language,
        i.e. children/young people.   *(1 mark)*

3   a)

Topic	Paragraph Number
Rules about the pizza	5
How the Margherita pizza got its name	9
A reaction from a top pizza chef	7
An introduction to the article	1

     1 correct paragraph   *(0 marks)*
     2 or 3 correct paragraphs   *(1 mark)*
     4 correct paragraphs   *(2 marks)*

     b) It has these different kinds of paragraphs because:
        the writer is trying to entertain as well as inform
        it shows a variety of ways of convincing the reader of the truth of the story.

(1 mark for either explanation)

4   Simple points made about the article, with limited awareness of how the writer tries to appeal to young people.   *(1 mark)*

Two examples of how the article is trying to appeal to young people, with some comment on how the text has this effect. Some awareness of effect is evident. Two of the three bullet points are addressed briefly.   *(2 marks)*

Shows some understanding of how facts and dates are used to make the article appeal to young people and an awareness of how the language and content affect the reader. Some references to the text are included to support ideas. The third bullet point is only briefly addressed.   *(3 marks)*

Some exploration of how the text tries to affect the reader through all three bullet points. A consistent attempt to comment on all three bullet points. References are used appropriately to support all ideas.   *(4 marks)*

A focused response which explores in detail, with close precise reference to the text, picking out individual words and phrases, how the article affects the reader. All three bullet points are addressed and a high level of awareness is shown by an understanding of different techniques that the writer has used.   *(5 marks)*

Oliver Twist

5 a) "suffered" or "tortures" (NOT "slow starvation" – the question says one word) *(1 mark)*

b) "suffered" – makes the reader think that they were in pain/had to put up with discomfort
"tortures" – makes the reader think that their pain was terrible/really bad/inflicted by someone else/on purpose
(1 mark for each valid response, linked to the answer to 5a)

6 It suggests that he is greedy. *(1 mark)*

7 a) Features of Oliver Twist's character from this extract:
He is brave (he accepts the challenge to ask for more/he accepts his beating)
He is persistent (he asks for more twice)
He doesn't care about his fate because he's so hungry
He is surprised by his own bravery
(1 mark for identifying any of the above)

b) Features of the master's character:
He is not used to being questioned or contradicted
He is easily angered
He is violent in nature
(1 mark for identifying any of the above)

8 a) It begins with long paragraphs and ends with shorter ones because:
The writer switches from narrative description to dialogue
The writer builds up the tension by describing the background first
(1 mark for either explanation)

b) It makes you feel sorry for Oliver because:
It is the second time he has had to ask
He is being well-mannered and reasonable and you would not expect anyone to refuse him
(1 mark for either explanation)

9 The writer wants us to feel sorry for Oliver. TRUE
The writer is trying to criticise the way that boys like Oliver were treated by authority. TRUE
The writer is trying to give a factual historical account. FALSE
The writer is trying to entertain the reader. TRUE

1 correct *(0 marks)*
2 – 3 correct *(1 mark)*
4 correct *(2 marks)*

Why is water good for you?

10 i It includes facts, e.g. "Water is extremely important for our bodies to work properly"
(1 mark – both reason and quotation needed)

ii It gives reasons, e.g. " ... because water is responsible for moving nutrients around the body"/"because ... most of the chemical reactions within our cells take place in water"
(1 mark – reason and either valid quotation needed, but quotation must include the word "because" up to a maximum of 2 marks)

11

Word/Phrase	Effect on the reader	How it creates this effect on the reader
We also lose water by evaporation	makes the reader think that drinking water is important	because it suggests that we need to replace this water
To stay healthy	makes the reader think that drinking water is important	because it suggests that you will be ill if you don't drink it
We should drink at least 6 to 8 cups	makes the reader think that drinking water is important	because it suggests that there is a great need for it

(1 mark for a quotation accompanied by an appropriate explanation, up to a maximum of 2 marks)

12 a) It acts as a diuretic.
You lose more water than normal.
It makes you need more water than normal.   *(1 mark for any of these responses)*

b) Brackets are used to <u>provide examples</u> of drinks that include caffeine.   *(1 mark)*

13 Simple points made about language or content, with limited awareness of how the writer tries to influence the reader.   *(1 mark)*

Two examples of how the language or content is making the article sound serious, with some comment on how the words influence the reader. Some awareness of effect is evident. Two of the three bullet points are addressed briefly.   *(2 marks)*

Shows some understanding of how the language and content make the article influence the reader. Some references to the text are included to support ideas. The third bullet point is only briefly addressed.   *(3 marks)*

Some exploration of how the language and content in the text try to influence the reader through all three bullet points. A consistent attempt to comment on all three bullet points. References are used appropriately to support all ideas.   *(4 marks)*

A focused response which explores in detail, with close precise reference to the text, picking out individual words and phrases, how the article affects the reader. All three bullet points are addressed and a high level of awareness is shown by an understanding of different techniques that the writer has used.   *(5 marks)*

Set B Answers – "Monsters" Reading Test Paper

Bigfoot of North America

1 • hairy
   • ape-like
   • biped
   • 7 – 9 feet tall
   • 600 – 900 pounds
   • 14" by 8" footprint size
   • 4 toes   *(1 mark for any of the above, up to a maximum of 2 marks)*

2 a) It suggests that:
      • It might not be true
      • There might have been earlier sightings that we don't know of
                              (1 mark for either of these responses)

   b) It suggests that:
      • They're unusual
      • They're not of a human or recognisable creature   *(1 mark for either of these responses)*

3 a)

Topic	Paragraph Number
A description of a captured Sasquatch	3
An introduction to what Bigfoot is	1
An explanation of what the captured Sasquatch might have been	4
The first sightings of a Sasquatch	2

   1 correct paragraph   *(0 marks)*
   2 or 3 correct paragraphs   *(1 mark)*
   4 correct paragraphs   *(2 marks)*

   b) • To make the passage more convincing
      • To show that the Bigfoot has been sighted by a variety of people
                              (1 mark for either of these responses)

4 Simple points made about how Bigfoot is a fake, with limited awareness of how the writer makes
   the reader feel this.   *(1 mark)*

   Two examples of how the article makes Bigfoot out to be a fake, with some comment on how the
   text has this effect. Some awareness of effect is evident. Two of the three bullet points are
   addressed briefly.   *(2 marks)*

   Shows some understanding of how historical examples are used to make the account believable
   and an awareness of how the descriptions of Bigfoot affect the reader. Some references to the
   text are included to support ideas. The third bullet point is only briefly addressed.   *(3 marks)*

Some exploration of how the text tries to affect the reader through all three bullet points. A consistent attempt to comment on all three bullet points. References are used appropriately to support all ideas. *(4 marks)*

A focused response which explores in detail, with close precise reference to the text, picking out individual words and phrases, how the article affects the reader. All three bullet points are addressed and a high level of awareness is shown by an understanding of different techniques that the writer has used. *(5 marks)*

Dracula

5 a) "for I did not know what to do" *(1 mark)*

b) Because s/he has to read on to find out what the narrator does. *(1 mark)*

6 It suggests that:
- They disapprove of the narrator
- They don't like him *(1 mark for either appropriate response)*

7 a) "The old man motioned me in ... with a courtly gesture" *(1 mark)*

b) Either of these quotations, or a summary of them, is acceptable:
- The man is unusually strong/"grasped mine with a strength which made me wince"
- The man does not seem alive or human/"more like the hand of a dead than a living man"
  (1 mark for an acceptable answer)

8 a) One mark for a difference that refers to both pairs of paragraphs – commenting on either paragraphs one and two or three and four alone gets no marks. The bit in brackets is not needed to get the mark – it is just to help you understand the answer.

Valid comments about paragraphs one and two:
- The writer uses lots of personal thoughts (to show us what he is thinking)
- The writer uses a lot of self-questioning (to show he is confused)

Valid comments about paragraphs three and four:
- The writer describes the old man from the narrator's viewpoint (so that we see him through his eyes)
- The writer describes the old man from the outside (so that we don't know what he's thinking, to make him more mysterious) *(1 mark)*

b) It makes the story interesting because it:
- Creates a sense of mystery
- Makes us want to read on to find out who he is *(1 mark for either valid comment)*

9 The writer wants us to feel that the narrator is confident. *FALSE*
The writer's aim is to entertain and interest the reader. *TRUE*
The writer wants us to like the old man. *FALSE*
The writer's aim is to build up tension in the reader. *TRUE*

1 correct *(0 marks)*
2 – 3 correct *(1 mark)*
4 correct *(2 marks)*

The Loch Ness Monster

10 "The Loch Ness Monster is <u>supposedly</u> living in Scotland's Loch Ness"
"this <u>unidentified</u> animal"
"a <u>strange</u> aquatic creature"
     (1 mark for identifying two of the above, up to a maximum of 2 marks for explanations of why these examples create a feeling of mystery – see the question)

11

Word/Phrase	Effect on the reader	How it creates this effect on the reader
convinced	makes the reader think that there might be some truth in the monster stories	because it suggests that the men had no doubts/believed what they saw
received several letters	makes the reader think that there might be some truth in the monster stories	because it suggests that the account made other people confess their experiences/come out with stories
claiming also to have seen	makes the reader think that there might be some truth in the monster stories	because it suggests that the account was backed up by other witnesses/other people had seen it

(1 mark for a quotation accompanied by an appropriate explanation, up to a maximum of 2 marks)

12 a) The writer uses the word "thorough" because:
- It suggests that the scientists had done their job properly
- It suggests that the entire loch has been surveyed   *(1 mark for either response)*

b) It is in inverted commas because the writer is casting doubt on whether the monster deserves to be called a monster/whether it really is a monster.   *(1 mark for either response)*

13 Simple points made about language or content, with limited awareness of how the writer tries to make it sound serious.   *(1 mark)*

Two examples of how the language or content makes the article sound serious, with some comment on how the words affect the reader. Some awareness of effect is evident. Two of the three bullet points are addressed briefly.   *(2 marks)*

Shows some understanding of how the language and content make the article sound serious. Some references to the text are included to support ideas. The third bullet point is only briefly addressed.   *(3 marks)*

Some exploration of how the language and content in the text try to affect the reader through all three bullet points. A consistent attempt to comment on all three bullet points. References are used appropriately to support all ideas.   *(4 marks)*

A focused response which explores in detail, with close precise reference to the text, picking out individual words and phrases, how the article affects the reader. All three bullet points are addressed and a high level of awareness is shown by an understanding of different techniques that the writer has used.   *(5 marks)*

Set C Answers – "Down South" Reading Test Paper

Jean Lafitte

1   He established his own kingdom of Barataria.
He claimed to command more than 1000 men/provided them as troops for the Battle of New Orleans.
He engaged in the slave trade after it was banned.   *(1 mark for each up to a maximum of 2)*

2   a) He had a varied life/it contained a mixture of exciting/good/bad incidents.
               (1 mark for an answer containing either of these explanations)

      b) His life has been exaggerated/his life is legendary
               (1 mark for an answer containing either of these explanations)

3   a)

Topic	Paragraph Number
The end of Jean Lafitte's life	6
Two places that exist today, connected to Jean Lafitte	7
A summary of Jean Lafitte's main achievements	1
The history of a diary about Jean Lafitte	3
A place named after Jean Lafitte	8
Reasons why Jean Lafitte became famous	4

    1 correct paragraph   *(0 marks)*
    2 or 3 correct paragraphs   *(1 mark)*
    4 correct paragraphs   *(2 marks)*

      b) Because it's writing to inform/it's from a reference book/encyclopaedia.
               (1 mark for an answer containing either of these explanations)

4   Simple points made about Jean Lafitte, with limited awareness of how the article tries to give the reader a fair view.   *(1 mark)*

    Two examples of how the article gives the reader a fair view, with some comment on how the text has this effect. Some awareness of effect is evident. Two of the three bullet points are addressed briefly.   *(2 marks)*

    Shows some understanding of how facts and dates are used to make the account believable and an awareness of how the descriptions of Jean Lafitte and his life affect the reader. Some references to the text are included to support ideas. The third bullet point is only briefly addressed.   *(3 marks)*

    Some exploration of how the text tries to affect the reader through all three bullet points. A consistent attempt to comment on all three bullet points. References are used appropriately to support all ideas.   *(4 marks)*

A focused response which explores in detail, with close precise reference to the text, picking out individual words and phrases, how the article affects the reader. All three bullet points are addressed and a high level of awareness is shown by an understanding of different techniques that the writer has used.

(5 marks)

Arriving In New Orleans

5   a) coasted

(1 mark)

   b) That the roar is either:
   • hideous
   • frightening
   • suggesting that something is being killed or badly hurt

(1 mark for any of these acceptable responses)

6   They were eager to see their destination.

(1 mark)

7   It is smelly/"odour of mud"/"fetid stink of cesspools"/"smell of burning sugar".
   It is crowded/"teeming streets"/"noisy, thronged streets".
   It is derelict/"only charred timbers among rampant fireweed".
   The people are unfriendly/"The man did not answer, spat to his right".

(1 mark for any two of the above up to a maximum of 2 marks. Quotations or explanations are acceptable for a mark)

8   a) Getting off the boat.

(1 mark)

   b) There is an emphasis on bad things, e.g. the cow bogged in the mud, the smell.
      There are hints of fear – the "quivering ship", the "gruesome roar", the "red moon crawled".

(1 mark for including one of the above reasons in the answer. No mark for an explanation not backed up with an example or quotation)

New Orleans

9   The writer wants us to be aware that New Orleans is a smelly place   TRUE
    The writer wants the reader to feel like the accordion maker   TRUE
    The aim of the writer is to scare the reader   FALSE
    The aim of the writer is to put people off visiting New Orleans   FALSE

   1 correct   *(0 marks)*
   2 – 3 correct   *(1 mark)*
   4 correct   *(2 marks)*

10   "seduces" – makes it sound like the place is chatting you up/enticing you/drawing you in like a lover.
    "sultry southern heat" – makes it sound sexy or steamy/alliteration "sultry southern" used to create a hot, steamy effect.
    "Caribbean colour" – it makes it seem lively and exotic/alliteration "Caribbean colour" used to create a lively effect.

(1 mark for each explanation supported by a quotation from this list of acceptable responses up to a maximum of 2 marks)

11

Word/Phrase	Effect on the reader	How it creates this effect on the reader
Enshrouding us in dreams	makes the reader think that New Orleans is exciting	because it suggests that it is a place of mystery/fantasy
sweet-tasting cocktails	makes the reader think that New Orleans is exciting	because it suggests that you can enjoy drinks that are better tasting/than in other places
laissez les bons temps rouler	makes the reader think that New Orleans is exciting	because it suggests that it is a party town/where people are just out to enjoy themselves
laced with voodoo potions	makes the reader think that New Orleans has a darker side	because it suggests that evil and black magic might affect you there without your knowledge
a well-earned reputation for excess and debauchery	makes the reader think that New Orleans has a darker side	because it suggests that people get out of control
The City That Care Forgot	makes the reader think that New Orleans has a darker side	because it suggests that the place is run down and abused

(1 mark for a quotation accompanied by an appropriate explanation, up to a maximum of 2 marks)

12 a) Because a checkerboard has a mix of black and white squares, just as New Orleans has a mix of contrasting neighbourhoods. *(1 mark)*

b) Because it's an explanation of the French word that comes before it. *(1 mark)*

13 Simple points made about language, with limited awareness of how the article tries to make it sound an exciting place. *(1 mark)*

Two examples of how the language makes the article exciting, with some comment on how the words affect the reader. Some awareness of effect is evident. Two of the three bullet points are addressed briefly. *(2 marks)*

Shows some understanding of how the language makes New Orleans sound lively and mysterious. Some references to the text are included to support ideas. The third bullet point is only briefly addressed. *(3 marks)*

Some exploration of how the language in the text tries to affect the reader through all three bullet points. A consistent attempt to comment on all three bullet points. References are used appropriately to support all ideas. *(4 marks)*

A focused response which explores in detail, with close precise reference to the text, picking out individual words and phrases, how the article affects the reader. All three bullet points are addressed and a high level of awareness is shown by an understanding of different techniques that the writer has used. *(5 marks)*

Writing Test Papers

The bands for writing give descriptions of the main features to look out for in your writing. Different bands have different amounts of marks in them.

For bands with three different marks, check the following.

- If your writing fits everything in that band, but shows no evidence of the bands above or below, give yourself the middle mark.

- If your writing fits everything in that band, but shows one piece of evidence of lower bands, give yourself the lower mark in the band.

- If your writing fits everything in that band, but shows one piece of evidence of higher bands, give yourself the higher mark in the band.

For bands with two marks, you need to do two of the things in the band to get the lower mark and everything in the band to get the higher mark.

For bands with one mark, you need to do everything in that band to get that mark.

It is important to look at the different marks you are getting in order to build up an accurate picture of the strengths and weaknesses of your writing – for example, you might get high marks on Composition and effect, but your spelling may be letting you down. If you know this, then you should focus on these areas when revising for your SATs.

Long Writing Task – Mark Scheme For All Papers

Section A: Sentence structure and punctuation

Band A1
Sentences and phrases are mostly linked with joining words like "and", "but" and "when".
Sentences are simple and may contain lots of repeated words and phrases.
Full stops, capital letters and exclamation marks are used to punctuate sentences,
mostly accurately.   *(0 marks)*

Band A2
Sentences are varied, and more complex joining words like "who" and "which" are used.
Words like "if" and "because" are used to help give reasons and for emphasising ideas.
Commas are used quite accurately within sentences.   *(1 or 2 marks)*

Band A3
Simple and more complex sentences are used – long sentences and short sentences are
used successfully.
Suggestions are given, by using words like "can" or "would".
A variety of punctuation is used with accuracy.
Different types of sentences, e.g. commands, questions or exclamations, are used in
order to create more interesting effects.   *(3 or 4 marks)*

Band A4

The writer begins sentences more skilfully, with words like "usually", "hopefully" etc. or by being impersonal, e.g. "Some people believe that ...".

A range of punctuation is used and this is sometimes done for deliberate effect, e.g. brackets are used to put in asides and thoughts. *(5 or 6 marks)*

Band A5

Sentences are varied, depending on the effect that the writer wishes to create.

Simple sentences might be used, but to create effects, e.g. shock or surprise.

Punctuation is used skilfully in order to make the reader speed up and slow down and to make the meaning of the writing perfectly clear. *(7 marks)*

Band A6

A wide range of sentence types is used with skill, accuracy and thought to control the writing.

There might be some non-standard sentences, but used for deliberate effect.

There is a very wide range of different types of punctuation used, in order to create a number of different effects. *(8 marks)*

Section B: Text structure and organisation

This section focuses on how overall meaning and effect is put across through the way that the writing is organised and planned.

Band B1

Ideas are mainly linked because they happen to be on the same topic.

Points might be put in a list, but not necessarily in any sort of order of importance.

Paragraphs might be used to show some of the obvious different topics in the writing. *(0 marks)*

Band B2

Paragraphs usually start with the main topic in the first sentence.

Paragraphs contain examples.

The writing has some brief opening and closing comments, but they will be fairly brief and undeveloped. *(1 or 2 marks)*

Band B3

Paragraphs are written in a logical order.

The introduction and conclusion are clear.

Paragraphs of different lengths are used, e.g. short paragraphs might take the form of a persuasive question. *(3 or 4 marks)*

Band B4

Detailed content is well handled within and between paragraphs.

Some phrases like "On the other hand" or "In addition to this" etc. are used to link the paragraphs.

The introduction and conclusion to the letter are developed and help to make it more persuasive. *(5 or 6 marks)*

Band B5

Paragraphs are varied in length to suit the different ideas being discussed.

Paragraphs are linked with a variety of words and phrases.

Paragraphs are ordered in such a way that the writer might have used them to highlight contrasts, or to be ironic. *(7 marks)*

Band B6

The whole piece of writing is organised, shaped and controlled to achieve a range of effects, or to get the reader thinking in a certain way.

Within paragraphs, the writer has used a wide range of links that are precisely and carefully chosen.

(8 marks)

Section C: Composition and effect

This section focuses on the overall impact of the writing and the effect it has on the reader.

Band C1

The writing shows some awareness of the reader.

There is some relevant content.

(0 marks)

Band C2

The writing is generally lively and attempts to interest the reader.

The content of the writing shows that the writer recognises its purpose.

Some reasons are given for the ideas and opinions, but perhaps not that many.

(1, 2 or 3 marks)

Band C3

The writing is detailed and gives clear reasons for the opinions and viewpoints expressed.

The writing engages the reader's interest.

The writing gives a range of relevant ideas and the writer's viewpoint is clear.

(4, 5 or 6 marks)

Band C4

The piece is well written because it uses a range of techniques such as repetition, humour and a consideration of the reader's needs in order to persuade.

The writer's view is consistent.

(7, 8 or 9 marks)

Band C5

The tone and content of the writing are appropriate and well judged.

The writing deliberately interacts with the reader.

Content is relevant throughout and is used to support the ideas.

(10, 11 or 12 marks)

Band C6

The writing has been done skilfully and the writer is totally in control of the writing type.

The viewpoint of the writer has been maintained throughout.

There is a strong individual style, created by a range of methods.

(13 or 14 marks)

Short Writing Task – Mark Scheme For All Papers

Section D: Sentence structure, punctuation and paragraph organisation

This section focuses on how you choose to organise your writing and how this contributes to its overall effect.

Band D1

Sentences are fairly simple.
Sentences are linked by simple joining words like "and" or "then".
Full stops and capital letters are used with accuracy.
Paragraphs are used to separate the more obvious different topics given in the task.   *(0 marks)*

Band D2

Sentences are varied and use linking words like "who" or "which".
The writing is written in the same tense throughout.
Words like "he", "she", "it," "they" and other pronouns are generally used correctly.
Paragraphs are mainly put into a logical order, as is the detail within them.   *(1 or 2 marks)*

Band D3

A variety of longer sentences is used. This includes those sentences that have been built up from joining simpler ones together to make longer ones and sentences where the word order has been successfully re-arranged for effect.
Words like "completely", "partly" and others which help to make meaning more precise, are used.
Words like "he", "she", "it", "they" and other pronouns are used correctly.
Tenses are used correctly.
Paragraphs are used for appropriate reasons and are put into a logical order.
The detail in them is put into a logical order.   *(3 or 4 marks)*

Band D4

Sentences are written in a variety of ways to achieve interesting effects that suit the purpose of the writing.
A range of punctuation is used – sometimes to create effects!
Paragraphs are of different lengths and the information in them is organised cleverly to suit what is being written about.   *(5 marks)*

Band D5

There is a wide range of sentence structures that use a sophisticated range of verbs and tenses.
Within paragraphs, the writer has used a wide range of links that are precisely and carefully chosen.
There is a very wide range of punctuation used, in order to make meaning clear and create a range of effects.   *(6 marks)*

Section E: Composition and effect

This section is to do with the overall impact of your writing and how well it fits the audience you are writing for.

Band E1
The writing shows some awareness of the reader.
Simple techniques, like repetition, are used.
Content is relevant to the question, but might well be unevenly used. *(0 marks)*

Band E2
The writing tries to interest the reader.
Some techniques, e.g. use of adjectives, are used to help writing, but they might not be very imaginative. *(1, 2 or 3 marks)*

Band E3
The writer interests the reader.
The writer is clearly aware of what type of writing he/she is doing and for whom.
The tone of the writing is consistent throughout. *(4, 5 or 6 marks)*

Band E4
The writing is well written and convincing throughout.
The writer really engages the reader's interest.
There is a very good range of well-chosen details.
The viewpoint of the writer is consistent throughout. *(7, 8 or 9 marks)*

Band E5
The writing has been done skilfully and the writer is totally in control of the writing type.
The viewpoint of the writer has been maintained throughout.
There is a strong individual style, created by a range of methods. *(10 marks)*

Section F: Spelling

This section focuses on accuracy in spelling. Choose the section that best fits the writing.

Band F1
Simple words and those with more than one or two syllables are generally accurate. *(1 mark)*

Band F2
More complicated words that fit to regular patterns and rules are generally accurate. *(2 marks)*

Band F3
Most spelling, including irregular words, is accurate. *(3 marks)*

Band F4
Virtually all spelling, including complex words that don't fit to regular rules or patterns, is correct. *(4 marks)*

Shakespeare Test Papers – Mark Scheme

Macbeth

The mark bands apply to all three Macbeth questions.

Find the band that best fits your answer and for every point in that band that you achieve, give yourself one mark within that band, e.g. if you think you are in Band 4 and you have done two of the points, then you should give yourself 11 marks.

Band 1
A few simple facts and opinions about the extracts.
There may be some misunderstandings.
Parts of the extracts are retold or copied and answers may be only partly relevant.   *(1, 2 or 3 marks)*

Band 2
Contains a little explanation, showing some awareness of the needs of the question.
Comments are relevant but are mostly about the plot.
Some broad references to how Macbeth speaks.   *(4, 5 or 6 marks)*

Band 3
Some general understanding of the question, although some points might not be developed.
Some comments on the language that Macbeth uses.
Some points backed up with reference to the text.   *(7, 8 or 9 marks)*

Band 4
Some discussion of how the extracts relate to the question, even though all the ideas might not be of equal quality.
Awareness of Macbeth's use of language and its effects.
Most points backed up with references to the text.   *(10, 11 or 12 marks)*

Band 5
Clear focus on how the extracts relate to the question.
Good consistent comments on Macbeth's language and its effects.
Well-chosen quotations linked together to present an overall argument.   *(13, 14 or 15 marks)*

Band 6
Every quotation is analysed in depth in relation to the question.
Every quotation is commented on in terms of the language that Macbeth uses.
Individual words are picked out of quotations and linked into the overall argument. *(16, 17 or 18 marks)*

Useful quotations for Macbeth Set A

Act 3 Scenes 1 and 2
"Know Banquo was your enemy."
>Macbeth is using his friend's reputation to cover his own desires.

"every minute of his being thrusts
Against my near'st of life"
>Macbeth values his ambition above his former friend.

"Fleance his son, that keeps him company,
Whose absence is no less material to me
Than is his father's, must embrace the fate
Of that dark hour."
>Macbeth cares so little for Banquo, he even wants to kill his son.

"Let your remembrance apply to Banquo;
Present him eminence, both with eye and tongue:"
>He advises Lady Macbeth to speak well of Banquo, which shows his deceitful attitude towards his former friend.

Act 3 Scene 4
"Thou art the best o' the cut-throats:"
>Macbeth is delighted at his enemy's death – quite different from his regret towards Duncan's death.

"Thanks for that:
There the grown serpent lies; the worm that's fled
Hath nature that in time will venom breed,"
>Macbeth is happy that Banquo is dead, but he still hates him, as his son Fleance is still alive and might do him harm.

Useful quotations for Macbeth Set B

Act 3 Scene 2
"We have scotch'd the snake, not kill'd it:"
>Macbeth has doubts.

"we will eat our meal in fear and sleep
In the affliction of these terrible dreams"
>Macbeth is frightened of his own conscience.

"Duncan is in his grave;
After life's fitful fever he sleeps well;"
>Macbeth is jealous of those who have peace of mind.

"make our faces vizards to our hearts,
Disguising what they are."

Macbeth is prepared to be deceitful.

"O, full of scorpions is my mind, dear wife!
Thou know'st that Banquo, and his Fleance, lives."
    Macbeth is greedy for power.

"Things bad begun make strong themselves by ill."
    Macbeth is growing in his evil attitude.

Act 3 Scene 4

"Thou canst not say I did it: never shake
Thy gory locks at me."
    Macbeth is overcome by guilt and fear.

"now they rise again,
With twenty mortal murders on their crowns,
And push us from our stools:"
    Macbeth is feeling terrible guilt.

"Hence, horrible shadow!
Unreal mockery, hence!"
    Macbeth wants to ignore/forget what he's done as that's the only way he can deal with it.

Useful quotations for Macbeth Set C

Act 3 Scene 1

"Ay, in the catalogue ye go for men;"
    Macbeth has little respect for human life.

"I will put that business in your bosoms,
Whose execution takes your enemy off,"
    Macbeth is being deceitful, using the Murderers' motives to disguise his own greed.

"Both of you
Know Banquo was your enemy."
    Macbeth is deceiving himself.

"Within this hour at most
I will advise you where to plant yourselves;"
    He is using others to do his dirty work – perhaps a sign of cowardice or guilt towards his killing of Duncan.

"Fleance ...
... must embrace the fate
Of that dark hour."
    Macbeth is becoming ruthless and selfish.

Act 3 Scene 4

"'Tis better thee without than he within.
Is he dispatch'd?"
    He is enjoying the death of Banquo, unlike the death of Duncan.

"But now I am cabin'd, cribb'd, confined, bound in
To saucy doubts and fears."

    Macbeth is insecure in his own position as King. He is still mentally trapped by the witches' predictions.

"the worm that's fled
Hath nature that in time will venom breed,
No teeth for the present."

    Macbeth is prepared to bide his time and kill again when he's ready.

Henry V

The mark bands apply to all three Henry V questions.

Find the band that best fits your answer and for every point in that band that you achieve, give yourself one mark within that band, e.g. if you think you are in Band 4 and you have done two of the points, then you should give yourself 11 marks.

Band 1
A few simple facts and opinions about the extracts.
There may be some misunderstandings.
Parts of the extracts are retold or copied and answers may be only partly relevant.   *(1, 2 or 3 marks)*

Band 2
Contains a little explanation, showing some awareness of the needs of the question.
Comments are relevant but are mostly about the plot.
Some broad references to how Henry speaks.   *(4, 5 or 6 marks)*

Band 3
Some general understanding of the question, although some points might not be developed.
Some comments on the language that Henry uses.
Some points backed up with reference to the text.   *(7, 8 or 9 marks)*

Band 4
Some discussion of how the extracts relate to the question, even though all the ideas might not be of equal quality.
Awareness of Henry's use of language and its effects.
Most points backed up with references to the text.   *(10, 11 or 12 marks)*

Band 5
Clear focus on how the extracts relate to the question.
Good consistent comments on Henry's language and its effect on the audience.
Well-chosen quotations linked together to present an overall argument.   *(13, 14 or 15 marks)*

Band 6
Every quotation is analysed in depth in relation to the question and there is an evaluation.
Every quotation is commented on in terms of the language that Henry uses.
Individual words are picked out of quotations and linked into the overall argument. *(16, 17 or 18 marks)*

Useful quotations for Henry V Set A

Act 4 Scene 1

"but it is no English treason to cut
French crowns, and to-morrow the king himself will
be a clipper."

> Henry is showing that he is prepared to do what his men are doing – fight – which shows he has the common touch.

"What infinite heart's-ease
Must kings neglect, that private men enjoy!"

> Henry is aware of how great a responsibility he has, one that ordinary men do not carry.

"What drink'st thou oft, instead of homage sweet,
But poison'd flattery?"

> Henry is aware that people will say falsely pleasant things to him, just because he's the king.

Act 5 Scene 2

"The princess is the better Englishwoman."

> Henry is modest.

"I know no ways to mince it in love, but
directly to say 'I love you:'"

> Henry is aware of his limitations.

"If thou canst love a
fellow of this temper, Kate, whose face is not worth
sun-burning, that never looks in his glass for love
of any thing he sees there,"

> Henry gets our sympathy as a person, because he lacks vanity, which makes him a stronger king.

Useful quotations for Henry V Set B

Act 4 Scene 1

"I think the king is but a man, as I
am:"

> Henry has to live up to people's expectations, whatever they are.

"I
believe, as cold a night as 'tis, he could wish
himself in Thames up to the neck;"

> Henry has to put up with the fact that some people might doubt him.

"I would he were here alone; so should he be
sure to be ransomed,"

> Henry has to put up with the fact that some people just see him as a political tool and don't care for his feelings.

*"Now, if these men do not die well, it
will be a black matter for the king that led them to
it;"*

Henry has the pressure of having to make decisions about men's lives.

Act 5 Scene 2
"thou wouldst find me such a plain king"

Henry has to put up with people having unreasonably high expectations of him.

*"If I could win a lady at
leap-frog, or by vaulting into my saddle with my
armour on my back, under the correction of bragging
be it spoken. I should quickly leap into a wife."*

Henry has to make do with his own strengths and weaknesses.

*"he hath not the gift to woo in other
places:"*

It is not really fair to criticise Henry for something that he does not have the natural ability to do.

*"take
me; and take me, take a soldier; take a soldier,"*

People have to accept Henry for what he is.

Useful quotations for Henry V Set C

Act 4 Scene 1
*"his cause being
just and his quarrel honourable."*

Henry justifies himself, which helps others to understand why he does things.

*"you may call the
business of the master the author of the servant's
damnation: but this is not so:"*

Henry reasons with people who are considered of a lower status, which makes him a man of the people.

*"Besides, there is no
king, be his cause never so spotless, if it come to
the arbitrement of swords, can try it out with all
unspotted soldiers:"*

Henry realises that he can't solve problems on his own and he needs the help and support of others.

*"Every
subject's duty is the king's; but every subject's
soul is his own."*

Henry is willing to lead, but he is able to respect the individuality of those under his command.

Act 5 Scene 2
"But, before God,
Kate, I cannot look greenly nor gasp out my
eloquence, nor I have no cunning in protestation;"
  Henry's modesty helps him to gain his future wife's respect.

"I speak to thee plain soldier;"
  His honesty wins him trust.

"in loving me, you should love
the friend of France; for I love France so well that
I will not part with a village of it:"
  Henry has the skill to turn other people's arguments around to suit his own views.

Much Ado About Nothing

The mark bands apply to all three Much Ado About Nothing questions.

Find the band that best fits your answer and for every point in that band that you achieve, give yourself one mark within that band, e.g. if you think you are in Band 4 and you have done two of the points, then you should give yourself 11 marks.

Band 1
A few simple facts and opinions about the extracts.
There may be some misunderstandings.
Parts of the extracts are retold or copied and answers may be only partly relevant.   *(1, 2 or 3 marks)*

Band 2
Contains a little explanation, showing some awareness of the needs of the question.
Comments are relevant but are mostly about the plot.
Some broad references to how Benedick speaks or acts.   *(4, 5 or 6 marks)*

Band 3
Some general understanding of the question, although some points might not be developed.
Some comments on the language that Benedick uses or the effect of the plot on the audience.
Some points backed up with reference to the text.   *(7, 8 or 9 marks)*

Band 4
Some discussion of how the extracts relate to the question, even though all the ideas might not be of equal quality.
Awareness of Benedick's use of language and its effects.
Most points backed up with references to the text.   *(10, 11 or 12 marks)*

Band 5
Clear focus on how the extracts relate to the question.
Good consistent comments on Benedick's language and its effect on the audience.
Well-chosen quotations linked together to present an overall argument.   *(13, 14 or 15 marks)*

Band 6
Every quotation is analysed in depth in relation to the question and there is an evaluation.
Every quotation is commented on in terms of the language that Benedick uses, or the difference between what he doesn't know and what the audience know.
Individual words are picked out of quotations and linked into the overall argument. *(16, 17 or 18 marks)*

Useful quotations for Much Ado About Nothing Set A

Act 1 Scene 1

"I noted her not; but I looked on her."
 The audience would find the way that Benedick is twisting Claudio's question amusing.

*"only this commendation I can
afford her, that were she other than she is, she
were unhandsome; and being no other but as she is, I
do not like her."*
 Benedick's direct rudeness of opinion would shock and amuse the audience.

"Shall I never see a bachelor of three-score again?"
 Benedick's exaggeration would amuse the audience.

Act 2 Scene 3

*"Shall
we go seek Benedick, and tell him of her love?"*
 Here the audience knows of the trick being played, but Benedick doesn't, so they would find it amusing that he's being taken in by Don Pedro and Leonato's conversation.

*"This can be no trick: the
conference was sadly borne"*
 This is amusing because the audience know that it is a trick! It makes the situation ironic.

*"Love me!
why, it must be requited."*
 The audience will find it amusing that Benedick seems to have so quickly changed his attitude towards women.

*"No, the world must be peopled. When I said I would
die a bachelor, I did not think I should live till I
were married."*
 The audience will find it amusing because Benedick is convincing himself with exaggerations.

Useful quotations for Much Ado About Nothing Set B

Act 1 Scene 1

*"With Hero, Leonato's
short daughter."*
 Benedick's blunt response makes him seem stubborn and comical.

"I shall see thee, ere I die, look pale with love."
 Don Pedro sets up a challenge in the minds of the audience.

"prove that ever I lose more blood
with love than I will get again with drinking, pick
out mine eyes with a ballad-maker's pen and hang me
up at the door of a brothel-house for the sign of
blind Cupid."

    Benedick is setting himself up for a fall because of his exaggeration and stubbornness.

Act 2 Scene 3

"but most wonderful that she
should so dote on Signior Benedick, whom she hath in
all outward behaviors seemed ever to abhor."

    The trap is set and the audience wait to see how Benedick will react to the bait.

"I should think this a gull, but that the
white-bearded fellow speaks it: knavery cannot,
sure, hide himself in such reverence."

    The audience know Benedick has been conned and share in the joke being played on him.

"No; and swears she never will: that's her torment."

    Leonato makes the audience wonder if Benedick will take the bait.

"Then down upon her knees she falls, weeps, sobs,
beats her heart, tears her hair, prays, curses; 'O
sweet Benedick! God give me patience!'"

    The audience will be amused to see the effect that Claudio's exaggeration has on Benedick.

Useful quotations for Much Ado About Nothing Set C

Act 1 Scene 1

"or would you have me speak
after my custom, as being a professed tyrant to their sex?"

    Benedick speaks his mind and comes across as a male chauvinist.

"and being no other but as she is, I
do not like her."

    Benedick is blunt but comical.

"Shall I never see a bachelor of three-score again?"

    Benedick is witty and sarcastic.

Act 2 Scene 3

CLAUDIO
"And she is exceeding wise."
DON PEDRO
"In every thing but in loving Benedick."

    Benedick is made an object of fun, which gains the audience's sympathy a little.

"I love Benedick well; and I
could wish he would modestly examine himself, to see
how much he is unworthy so good a lady."

    The audience see that Benedick is taken in by compliments.

"This can be no trick: the
conference was sadly borne."

    The audience see that Benedick is gullible.

"Love me!
why, it must be requited."

    The quick change of heart amuses the audience by showing how love can affect anyone
    – even Benedick!

"I must not seem proud:"

    Benedick tries to be aware of his self-image, which might gain him some sympathy.

"but
doth not the appetite alter?"

    Benedick's justification for his change of heart amuses the audience because he's changed so much.